THE
BILLY MARTIN
STORY

Billy Martin's story is an inspiration to all boys striving to rise above their humble surroundings. He was born in the dock area of Berkeley, California, and at an early age found that he had to fight for the privilege of playing sandlot baseball. After four years with the minor clubs, he came to the Yankees and soon was the spark plug of the team, winning the Babe Ruth Memorial Trophy for his record-breaking 1953 World Series. Although he has been traded to several clubs, he continues to have the terrific pride, enthusiasm and unselfish dedication to baseball that make him the kind of player any manager would be proud to have on his team.

Books by Joe Archibald

THE BILLY MARTIN STORY

THE RICHIE ASHBURN STORY

Billy with Mickey Mantle, 1954

Shortstop Riz-
zuto works out
with rookie
Billy Martin,
spring training,
1950

Casey Stengel with World Series hero of 1953

Billy Martin,
Yankee second
baseman, 1951
←

Happy at opening game victory over Dodgers in 1953
World Series

Martin at Fort Ord, 1954

Receiving the Babe Ruth Award for his outstanding play in the 1953 World Series

Martin leaps over Bob Nieman of the Orioles to start a double play, 1956

Billy Martin playing third base for the Kansas City Athletics, 1957

Lois Berndt and Billy Martin, married on October 30, 1950

Billy Martin reunited with Tommy Henrich at Detroit Tigers spring training camp, 1958

THE BILLY MARTIN STORY

❖❖❖❖❖❖❖❖❖❖❖❖❖❖❖❖❖❖❖❖❖❖❖❖❖❖❖❖

BY JOE ARCHIBALD

JULIAN MESSNER, INC.
NEW YORK

Published by Julian Messner, Inc.
8 West 40th Street, New York 18
Published simultaneously in Canada
by The Copp Clark Publishing Co., Limited
© Copyright 1959 by Joe Archibald

Third Printing, 1962

Photographs used with the
permission of Wide World Photos

PRINTED IN THE UNITED STATES OF AMERICA
Library of Congress Catalog Card No. 59–7007

Chapter I

AT YANKEE STADIUM on the afternoon of July 12, 1952, tempers on the diamond were as hot as the sun. The majority of fans in the stands had been lured to the ball park by the promise of fireworks always ready to be touched off whenever the Bombers played the lowly St. Louis Browns. For there was a husky, bespectacled catcher with the visiting team named Clint Courtney, who had been waging a one-man feud against the Yankees from the first day he had suited up in Brownie livery.

The Yankees had once owned Courtney but had traded him to the Browns. The big backstop took this as a personal insult and decided he would get even with every man on the New York payroll, and his particular aversion and prime target seemed to be Billy Martin, the Bombers' brash little second baseman.

In the second inning Courtney stepped up to the plate, disdainful of the lusty booing of the fans and the sharp needling of the Yankee bench jockeys. Courtney was a blocky man and dangerous with his big bat. The Yankee infield moved back and a little around to the right. There was a noticeable arrogance in the way the St. Louis catcher studied the defense set up against him.

A Yankee on the bench yelled shrilly, "Stick it in his ear!"

"Right under the bum's chin!" a leather-lunged fan shouted.

Billy Martin looked over at shortstop Phil Rizzuto. The Scooter grinned back at him, but his eyes carried a warning: Look out for that Courtney!

"That's our boy!" Billy chirped. "Watch him!" He danced around, lifted his cap, and smoothed back his black curly hair. He looked up at the flags to see if the wind had changed direction. Studying the shift of Courtney's feet, he moved a little more to the right.

There was a gleam of anticipation in Billy's dark eyes. He was the holler guy for the Bombers. He was hollering now — and also remembering that Courtney had once called him "Dago" and had made uncomplimentary remarks about the size of his nose. But worst of all, and most unforgivable, was Courtney's inference that Billy Martin could not hit his way out of a paper bag.

The pitch went in. Billy uncoiled at the crack of Courtney's bat, but the ball was through the hole and out into right field. Courtney rounded first, hesitated for a moment, glanced at Billy covering the keystone sack, then took off for second. Billy took the throw-in and knew he had Courtney, no speedster, nailed. But Courtney hit the dirt with all of his one hundred and eighty-odd pounds and came in high. Billy did not back up an inch. He was hit hard and bowled over and the ball fell out of his glove. When he got up and brushed the dirt from him, Courtney said, "You got in my way, Billy boy. Watch that!"

Billy's olive-skinned face blazed with fury, but he quickly got control of his temper. He walked around until he had shaken off the effects of the violent contact. He banged dirt out of his glove and yelled at Courtney, "Keep coming. Just keep coming!"

The crowd finally stopped booing and settled back to wait for a bigger explosion.

In the sixth inning Courtney came up again and banged out his second single. A few minutes later, trying to score from third on Dyck's grounder to McDougald, he was out at the plate by nearly ten feet. But Courtney, with the ball already in Berra's big mitt, slid in hard. Yogi was knocked over, the sound of the impact carrying high into the stands. Unhurt, Berra got to his feet and said something to Courtney, but the St. Louis catcher turned a malicious grin toward Yogi, then walked to the dugout. The crowd was roaring mad.

"That guy is really asking for it today," Rizzuto said when the Yankees came in for their turn at bat.

"I'm waiting for that joker," Billy Martin said grimly. "Just let him come my way. I'll make him eat that ball."

"Just cool off," Casey advised. "You want to hit something, you fellas, knock out that pitcher."

The game went on. The sharp, acrid smell of fireworks was in the heat of the afternoon. The umpires were irritable and unusually grim jawed. They seemed to sense the impending rhubarb. Courtney kept ribbing the Bombers unmercifully as they came to the plate; the sputtering fuse kept shortening. In the eighth inning, with the Browns at bat, it reached the powder-keg stage.

Once again as Courtney stepped out of the batter's circle, Yankee rooters turned their displeasure on him. Dick Kryhoski, first baseman for the Browns, had reached first, but was quickly forced at second when Courtney drove a grounder to the infield. Big Clint took a short lead off the bag, his eyes fixed on Billy Martin. There was a cold grin on the big catcher's face. Anger still smoldering through him, Billy said to himself, "Come on down, Clint. I'll be waiting."

St. Louis strategy called for a delayed steal; Courtney got the sign and took off when the pitch was delivered. Berra quickly threw the ball down to second where Martin was waiting. Courtney was out by the proverbial mile as Billy took the ball with his bare hand, but the pugnacious catcher hit the dirt, his spikes high, trying to cut Billy down. Billy got clear, then tagged Courtney hard on the mouth for the third out, and walked toward the Yankee bench.

Courtney's roar of rage turned Billy around, and he saw the catcher rushing at him, his fists clenched. "You fresh Dago! I'll tear you apart, you —— "

Billy clamped his jaws tight and stood his ground. "Come and get it, tough guy!" he yelled and started swinging. He hit Courtney twice without a return, both punches landing on Courtney's jaw.

They closed like two battling bears and wrestled around. Bill Summers and Larry Knapp, rushing in to break it up, quickly found themselves on the ground. The fans were up and roaring. Both dugouts began to empty, Yankees and Browns swarming onto the field. Before order was restored, Allie Reynolds, Johnny Mize, Gil McDougald, Joe Collins of the Yankees, and Billy Hunter and several other Browns had thrown a flurry of punches.

Leaving the battleground with a convoy of delighted Yankees, Billy yelled, "Courtney started it, so I belted him! You let anybody get the best of you in this game and you're done!"

This was the warcry Billy Martin had brought from the wrong side of the tracks in Berkeley, California. It applied not only to the game of baseball but to every part of his life.

In the dugout, when play got under way again, Old Case passed a gnarled hand across the lower part of his rugged face as if wiping away a grin. He glanced at Billy Martin, admiration plain in his eyes. He had always called the second baseman his kind of ballplayer. Billy would fight at the drop of a hat. He was outrageously cocky and talkative as a cage of magpies. Not for one minute did he hesitate to tell Allie Reynolds or Ed Lopat how to pitch, or give advice to Yogi Berra when the slugging catcher went into a batting slump.

"Sure," Stengel thought, "I guess maybe I never should have given this fella so much rope — this fresh kid who's always sassing somebody and getting away with it. Maybe I shoulda kept him down more, quieted him some, I don't know . . . " The Yankees were out there hitting but he hardly saw them. His mind had drifted back to the old days when he managed the Oakland Acorns of the Pacific Coast League. One day Red Adams, the Oakland trainer, brought a sixteen-year-old gangly kid, dressed in an Oaks uniform, into the ball park.

"Case," Adams said, "I've got a hot prospect here. His name is Billy Martin."

"What?" Stengel roared. "That scarecrow? Why, he don't weigh ninety pounds soaking wet and with a loaded bat in each hand."

"Neither did Johnny Evers, Case. This kid has big hands and he's real fast. I wish you'd try him out."

"Go away," Casey said.

Billy's dark eyes shot sparks. "All right," he said, "but the day will come when I'm playing ball for you, Mr. Stengel."

"Which means them sea gulls out there in the bay will be chewing tobacco," Casey said.

A year went by and Red Adams brought Billy into the Oakland ball park again. He cornered Stengel and made him listen to the stories of Billy's exploits as a semipro with the James Kenney Playfield team at Berkeley. Much against his will, Stengel consented to hit some ground balls at the kid. He made it a point to smash them as hard as he could, yet Billy gloved them all cleanly, throwing the ball back at Stengel with all the strength he could get behind it.

After one stung Casey's hand he called a halt and said to Adams, "Okay, bring him around again, Red."

Sure, he finally signed Billy Martin to a contract and sent him to Idaho Falls in the Pioneer League. "You'll meet them as tough as you are out there," he told the rookie. "I just hope you'll come back alive."

From Idaho Falls the kid from the slums of Berkeley had gone to Phoenix, and in 1947 Casey brought him back to Oakland, where he prepared him for the Yankee uniform he was now wearing, even though the kid was more brash and impudent than ever. News of the many diamond battles Billy had been in came in ahead of him.

The last out was made and Casey came back to the present. Sure, a remarkable ballplayer, that fella Martin.

Chapter II

BERKELEY, CALIFORNIA is often referred to as a cultural center and a genteel residential suburb. It is built on hills and surrounded on three sides by the campus of the University of California. But, like most cities, it also has an ugly side. The slum section looks out over San Francisco Bay, its eyes the grimy windows of factories lining the docks of the eastern shore. The tenements with their peeling paint, sour smells, and untidy yards stretch out in monotonous sameness for several blocks away from the bay — a world in itself, as far removed from the more abundant life of the city as if it had been near the banks of the Nile.

On a night when the wind blew the clammy mist in off the bay, a boy stopped in front of a stationery store and stared at the headlines of an evening paper on a small wooden stand:

SEALS SWAMP ACORNS, 9–1

The boy's eyes were dark pools in a solemn face. His black hair was sadly in need of a barber's shears and

14

he had been given a little too much nose for such a little fellow. There was a cut on the bridge of it and it was bleeding. One of the knees of his baggy pants had been ripped open.

He started walking toward Seventh Street, then stopped as if he had reached a sudden and important decision. Turning abruptly, he walked in the direction from which he had come. A few minutes later he stood in front of St. Ambrose's Church, tucking his shirt inside his belt and drawing a sleeve across the cut on his nose. He hoped he would find Father Dennis Moore in.

"It's worth a try," the boy mumbled to himself. "It just might work." He walked up the steps of the rectory, pushed the bell, and waited. He was about to leave when the heavy wooden door swung open. When Father Moore peered out and recognized his visitor, a warm smile played on his kindly Irish face for a moment. Then he eyed the boy a bit suspiciously. "Billy, you did not come to sweep out the church today," he said. "Isn't it time you were home having supper?"

"Yes, Father. I thought — well — I ——"

"Come in, Billy," Father Moore said. "It seems you have something important on your mind."

The priest turned on some extra light after he seated the boy in a big leather chair. Studying his young caller for a moment, he sighed and shook his head. "Your knuckles are skinned, Billy Martin, and you have a cut on your nose. You have been fighting again."

"Yes, Father," Billy said sheepishly, but his dark eyes soon began to smolder. "Two kids bigger than me on

Fourth Street. They made fun of my nose and ears.
What made me fight, though, was their callin' me
Alfred."

Father Moore averted his gaze for an instant to hide
a smile. When he faced Billy again his face looked
stern. "It is your name, isn't it, Billy?"

"It was my father's name . . . I've never even seen
him," the boy said, his jaw thrust out. "I hate it. I'll
lick any kid that calls me Alfred."

"It is wrong to fight, Billy," Father Moore said. "But
I have told you that many times, haven't I? I must save
my breath. Now, Billy, tell me why you came to see me."

"I thought maybe you'd give me a food package to
take home, Father. I'd come very early tomorrow afternoon and work to pay for it."

Father Moore smiled, then shook his head. "No,
Billy. You know that isn't the right way. You mustn't
take something you haven't rightfully earned."

"But they'll punish me. They'll know I wasn't at the
church today."

"Punishment you must learn to accept," the priest
said, "if you really deserve it, Billy. I'm sorry."

The boy got up slowly from the big chair, a rueful
smile appearing at the corners of his mouth. "I sure
will get it good, specially from my grandmother. Well,
I'll be here early tomorrow, Father. I promise."

The priest laid a hand on his shoulder. "I believe
you, my son. Now you run on home."

Billy Martin hurried, although he knew full well
what was in store for him. The family lived in a sixty-

year-old two-story frame house on Seventh Street. As Billy walked in and closed the door softly behind him he heard his grandmother's voice and shuddered at its harshness. She spoke only in Italian, hardly knowing a word of English.

"Bellino! Is that you, Bellino?"

Billy swallowed hard, took a deep breath, then answered, "Yes, it is me, Nona." It was the name he had called her since he was old enough to make himself understood. He smelled the meat sauce for the spaghetti cooking in the kitchen and heard his baby sister Joan crying.

His mother called from the kitchen, "Billy, where on earth have you been? Have you brought the food package from the church?"

He tried to answer but his throat tightened up. And then Nona, the grandmother he both feared and deeply loved, was standing in front of him, her hands on her hips, her old but lively eyes sweeping him from dark unruly hair to scuffed shoes. He had always believed she could read his innermost thoughts, and only once had he tried to outwit her.

"After school, Bellino, you did not go to St. Ambrose's. Instead, you were fighting in the streets again. You are a bad boy, Bellino. The devil must be driven out of you."

"Yes, Nona."

The punishment never varied. His grandmother hit him on the back of the head with the flat of her hand. She took him by the shoulders and shook him until his teeth rattled. She slapped him hard where he sat down and then said, "Now, Bellino, you will go into the front room and say your prayers in Italian."

The family was already seated at the big table when he finished his penance. His brother Jackie sat on his stepfather's knee, the lower part of his face already stained with marinara sauce. His stepfather Jack Downey said, "Billy, you must stop this fighting. You want to be a ballplayer and nowadays they are not roughnecks — you remember that." He spoke with effort, for his asthma plagued him. The ailment prevented him from holding a steady job, and so the food packages Billy earned at St. Ambrose's were sorely needed.

Billy's conscience nagged him as he ate. He looked over at his mother, his dark eyes searching for a sign of forgiveness. She was a tiny woman, still very pretty. She had been born Joan Salvini, the daughter of an Italian fisherman who had come to San Francisco in the 1870's. Billy felt much better when his mother smiled at him. Tomorrow, the next day, and the next he would work hard. Someday he would be a great ballplayer and make a lot of money. Then he would dress Nona and his mother in fine clothes. He'd fix up the house like a palace too, and send Joan to a fine school.

"When you are through, Bellino," Nona said, "you take off your pants and I mend them. Your soul should be as easy fixed, eh?"

Billy grinned at his grandmother, and her face broke into a sunny, tolerant smile. He rubbed his bruised knuckles against the side of his leg and chuckled to himself. He sure had tagged that long-legged kid with the birthmark on his cheek. No wonder he worshipped Nona. But for her he would have had to fight every kid in an area of six square blocks. They had heard her call him Bellino — the Italian word for handsome — and they all thought she meant Billy. If they only knew what his real name was — Alfred Manuel Martin. He wrinkled his nose at the thought of it.

Despite the opinions of most of the people in the slum district, Nona believed in her grandson's ultimate success. "You will see," she always said, "Bellino will be a great ballplayer."

Billy shared a room with her. She did not mind his cluttering up his part of it with souvenirs found during his expeditions to the docks, dark alleys, and vacant lots. He had pictures of famous ballplayers all over his old dresser, and when he told her about them, she smiled and nodded as if she really understood.

"That one is Ty Cobb," he explained one night. "The best player of them all, they say. Cobb said the base path belongs to the runner and if a baseman gets in the way he should be knocked down. He made more base hits than any other man in the history of the game. But it was the Bambino who — — "

"Ah, the Bambino — Ruth, Bellino. She is the one I like to hear about."

"Ruth was a *he*," Billy corrected her, smiling.

She would tell him about faraway Italy before he fell asleep, about the vineyards and the olive trees.

Once she had gone to Rome to see the Vatican. But when Billy asked about his father, and why he had gone away from the house on Seventh Street and never come back, she would always change the subject.

"You are too young to talk of such things, Bellino," she said.

THERE IS NO POETRY in the coming and going of the seasons near the docks of San Francisco Bay. To Billy Martin even these seemed hand-me-downs from the richer sections of the city. Every free moment when he was not working to help keep food on the family table, he played ball in the streets and empty lots. Although more often than not he had to fight for the privilege, with a bat in his hand he felt equal to any other boy in the community. When he swung it and connected solidly, he was hitting back at the world. Out in the field he derived a fierce satisfaction from stopping the vicious drives aimed his way.

Baseball was Billy's sanctuary, his way of belonging. Empty soda bottles which were found or given to the kids of the neighborhood were turned in for enough cash to purchase twenty-five-cent baseballs. After an hour of playing they were lopsided and losing their stuffing. The cheap bats — all they could afford — splintered easily and the imitation-leather gloves fell apart. But to Billy the glamour and excitement of the game was as intense there as at any big-league stadium. When he drove the ball clear out of the lot, he imagined fifty thousand people were cheering him, and his shrill voice was heard above all the others. Once Father Moore told his mother, "He wouldn't ever dare to lie about playing baseball. I hear him when I stand out in front of the church."

Billy nearly tore a sandlot game apart the year before he was to enter high school. His side was losing. He knew the freckled-faced kid on the pitching mound was no longer trying after four runs had been scored off him in the top of the sixth inning, so Billy came in from shortstop and told him to throw harder.

"Aw, they hit everything I throw," the pitcher said.

"So could my grandmother," Billy said in disgust. "Get going now, put some beef behind that ball!"

The kid on the mound wound up lazily and threw a slow ball. The batter hit it over second base — and another run scored. Billy ran in and pushed the pitcher off the hill. When he yelled for another boy to take over the pitching, three of the pitcher's close friends swarmed toward him. Billy dug in and faced them all. "I hate anybody that don't try!" he said angrily. "I hate a guy who *likes* to lose. Come on, who wants to throw the first punch?"

One boy tried and Billy knocked him down. Both teams swung into action, threatening a free-for-all, but Father Moore and several other older fans moved in to break it up.

"Maybe he was doing the best he could," the priest said to Billy.

"No, he wasn't, Father. He quit. Show me a quitter and I'll show you a coward."

"You like to win, don't you, Billy?"

Billy grimly nodded.

"You've got to lose many times in this life," Father Moore pointed out.

"Sure, but I'll always put up a fight, Father."

Father Moore walked away with a tall, gray-haired man. "That boy will go a long way from this slum district," he said. "With the proper guidance . . . with a little humility . . . " Then he grinned. "What am I saying?"

Going to high school in Berkeley was a frightening thought. Billy would meet the boys and girls from families that never knew hard times, and he wondered if they would accept him. They would wear nice clothes and their manners would be just right. The week before school opened in September, Billy tried to persuade Nona and his mother to let him go to work. The family needed his support, he insisted desperately.

"I'll get a steady job, Nona. In a year or so I'll be getting paid for playing baseball too. On nights and weekends. I'll make lots of money."

"Did you hear this crazy Bellino?" the old lady asked. "I should box his ears, eh? You will go to school and learn, Bellino, and shut your mouth on any more such foolish talk. All your clothes I have cleaned and mended!"

"I'll look like a ragbag beside most of those kids," Billy protested. He picked up his old sweater and saw where Nona had mended the elbows. He threw it down. "Someday I'll have twenty suits of clothes! I'll wear silk shirts — and I'll have a dozen pairs of shoes!"

"More crazy talk," his grandmother said, her sharp eyes beginning to snap. "I should feel your head for fever, no?"

Billy hastily retreated. The storm signals in Nona's eyes were plain. Outdoors, he found his stepfather sitting on the steps. "You know your grandmother is right, Billy," Jack Downey said. "You don't want to be a nobody like me, do you? In high school they have a baseball coach and he'll teach you what you need to know about the game. That's what you want most, isn't it?"

"Sure."

"Don't be afraid of the other kids," Downey went on. "Most people, I have found, will meet you halfway in this world. What do you say about going duck hunting tomorrow? Bring one of your friends."

"Now you're talking," Billy said.

They went over to Point Isabelle on the bay the next morning. Downey had built an old blind near the shore and they waited there until the mists began to clear. Far down shore they heard gunshots and Downey said, "Lot of sky-busters out today, like always. They fire pounds of lead but always miss."

"Like a wild swinger in baseball," Billy said. "They'll cut at anything."

Downey got in some shots, but no birds fell. There was a lot of shooting all around them and after it had quieted down, Billy and his friend went down to an old raft they had left in the reeds. They poled it up and down the shore looking for ducks other hunters had hit but failed to find. It turned out to be one of Billy's lucky days. He found a mallard and a pintail, both good and fat, and in his excitement he nearly fell into the water twice on the way back.

"Wow!" his stepfather exclaimed. "You made a haul, Billy. But Nona will skin you. You're soaked and your shoes are full of mud."

"Maybe," Billy said. "But these will taste good afterward." The somberness came into his dark face as they started homeward. Always, it seemed, the family lived on leftovers. Even these plump ducks really belonged to someone else. Sure, they were hand-me-downs.

Chapter III

BILLY MARTIN made shortstop on the Berkeley High School team. Although he was the smallest player, he more than held his own, both at bat and in the field. But it did not take players of other high schools long to hit him where he hurt the most. "Pinocchio!" they yelled when they wanted to drive him wild. Oversensitive about his big nose, he cracked wide open when the taunts built up.

Fred Moffett, the Berkeley coach, took Billy out of a game one afternoon when he threw down his tattered glove and charged the other team's third-base coach. He let his fists fly at the bigger kid and soon had him in the dust. The combined efforts of five other players were needed before Billy was subdued.

He went to the locker room and sat down on the bench, tears in his eyes. He did not take off his uniform. Going home at this time of day would require an explanation, one that could lead to drastic measures on the part of Nona. She had been sparing with her hands of late, but she kept her tongue very sharp. During the game he had been somebody. Here, he was nothing. He was still in the locker room, just beginning to take off his uniform, when the team filed in. By the way they were laughing and horsing around, Billy knew Berkeley had won. Babe Van Heuit, one of their star players, said laughingly, "You must have shaken that coach up, Billy. He waved a man around third when the ball was practically in the catcher's mitt."

The coach yelled at Billy: "You still here? You've been sitting around in that wet uniform?"

He nodded.

"After you've showered, I want to see you, Martin."

The other players left Billy alone. They were warned by the set of his jaw, the gleam in his dark eyes.

Later Billy walked into the coach's office just off the locker room. Moffett said sternly, "Sit down, Martin," then studied the shortstop for a long moment. The anger in him quickly faded, for he remembered things he had heard about this boy from Seventh Street. "I understand you want to be a big-league ballplayer, Billy," he began.

"I will be too. Nobody will stop me."

"They will if you don't get straightened out. What do they call a player who can't take a ribbing? They call him rabbit ears. More than one great prospect has been run out of the big leagues because of them — and not just curve balls."

"I'll take just so much, Coach, but there's a limit to everything."

"You should have heard them ride the Babe. Cobb, Speaker, Hornsby — all the greats had to take the barrage from the visitors' bench. Look, you're a good ballplayer, Martin, if you'll learn to control your temper.

Aggressiveness is a good thing, but it has to be controlled. We expect all boys playing for Berkeley to be gentlemen."

"You won't find many where I come from, Coach," Billy said stubbornly. "Go over to Seventh Street sometime and watch them play ball. Any kid that hates a fight stays away."

"A test of real character, Martin," the coach pursued, "is rising above that kind of crowd." He studied the boy closely, then made a gesture of impatience. "All right, I'll forget this latest outburst. But watch yourself or you'll be off this team."

Billy nodded, his lips stretched tight.

He became known as the best shortstop in the City League, enduring merciless riding from the spectators and rival players with only an occasional mild flare-up. It required all of his will power to hold these to a minimum of fireworks.

Billy took no part in the social life of Berkeley High School. When he was not playing baseball or struggling with his books, he was working at odd jobs. One day Babe Van Heuit met him on the front steps of the school. "Billy, there's a dance Saturday night at the gym," he said. "I've got a girl for you. Just your size. You should try and mix more."

Billy shook his head and grinned ruefully. "I never learned to dance. If I'd tried, I'd have been killed over by the docks. Girls? I don't know how to talk to one. And I haven't the right clothes, Babe. When they run a party where we wear baseball suits, let me know."

"I'll bet your heart is covered with horsehide, Billy, and stitched like a ball."

"And glove padding for brains," Billy added. "I'm sure glad this is my last year in high school."

"We should take the league championship this year. With you in there, we can't miss." Babe laughed "It's sure a kick watching the coach every time you look on the verge of flying off the handle. They say you're giving him an ulcer."

"They won't get my goat any more," Billy said. "Tell that girl if she wants a blind date I know an umpire who —— "

Van Heuit went away laughing.

Three weeks later, however, came a big explosion. The abuse from opposing players had been steadily building up inside Billy until there was room for no more. Berkeley was playing Hayward High, and their rivalry had been intense for years. Hayward rooters, their team behind, taunted every Berkeley player as he came up to hit. There was a runner on first when Billy walked to the plate, boasting a remarkable .470 batting average. Quickly the Hayward bench and the spectators in the stands turned loose on the little shortstop.

"Yeah, Pino-o-o-occhio-o-o-o-o!"

"Jug ear-r-r-r-r-rs! How do you walk against the wind?"

"Schnozzola Durante!"

Billy took a called strike, his temper heating up. He reached down for some dirt and a Hayward player shouted, "And get the spaghetti out of your ears, Martin!"

He set his jaws tight and waited for the next pitch, fighting to keep control.

"Brush his nose back!" somebody yelled at the pitcher, and then Billy threw his bat away and charged the Hayward rooting section. He swung his fists wildly and before he was immobilized there were bloodied noses and puffed lips. Fred Moffett got hold of Billy and ordered him off the field. "Turn in your suit immediately!" he shouted at the shortstop.

More angry at himself than anyone else, Billy headed for the showers. The tears burned hot in his eyes as he slammed the door of the locker room shut behind him. The boos of the fans still rang in his ears. He took off his cap and threw it across the room, then sat down on the wooden bench and pounded his fists against his knees. He was finished this time. He would never get another chance with Moffett.

He had to tell Nona. It would be all over town by nightfall. He sat there planning the things he would say to her, but soon gave up, for he knew she understood him better than he did himself. He undressed slowly, a hard lump in his throat, knowing he would never see the inside of this room again. It was his world. It smelled of the liniment used to ease hard knocks. He showered, got into his everyday clothes, then hung up his uniform in a locker bearing his name. "When I put on another monkey suit," he told himself, "I'll get paid for it."

When Billy got home he said to Nona, "I got into a big fight — they fired me off the team."

His grandmother's lively eyes showed signs of anger,

but quickly softened. He looked utterly lost and forlorn. "Ah, Bellino," she said, rumpling his dark hair, "I guess you will never never change. But maybe this will teach you a good lesson, eh? So they don't want my Bellino no more? Someday they will. Someday you will be a famous ballplayer."

"You get washed, Billy," his mother said. "Tonight we have veal scallopini."

"I've already had a wash." He crossed the room and picked up his little sister Joan. "When you go to high school you will go to dances and have pretty dresses, I promise," he told her. "Nobody will ever make fun of you."

"One thing she will do without being told," Nona said. "She will study hard. That is something you never do, Bellino."

Billy admitted it. Only a few days ago he had been told that his marks were bad. The principal had hinted strongly that he would not be allowed to play baseball unless he improved. One way or another, it seemed, the odds had been stacked against him.

After supper he took a walk. As he passed St. Ambrose's, Father Moore was out in front of the church talking to the policeman on the beat. "Well, how did it go today, Billy?" the priest called out.

"Not so good, Father," Billy said, eying the officer warily. He had been chased by this man more than once.

"I'll say it didn't," the policeman said. "Father, haven't you heard? This kid nearly caused a riot. He tore into the whole Hayward High rooting section and sure left his mark on some people. Someday I'm afraid he'll get into some real serious trouble." He threw Billy a stern glance and went on his way.

Father Moore said softly, "You'd better come in and tell me about it." There was no impatience, no trace of censure, in his voice. He knew the boy. He knew, too, that life had made him vulnerable.

Billy sank down in the familiar chair in the priest's study. "Father," he said, "I knew I was doing wrong, but something just blew up inside me. I just had to fight back. I know the Bible says to turn the other cheek. But after that, what does a guy do?"

Father Moore smiled tolerantly and shook his head from side to side. "Maybe God never played baseball, Billy. He possibly would have laid down some special rules for ballplayers if He had."

A small smile passed over the boy's face, then he became deadly serious again. "They don't know, guys like Coach Moffett, Father," he said. "They weren't ever kicked around." He bent far forward in his chair and stared down at the floor. "If you let them get the best of you, you're done!"

"Well, Billy, it seems you let them get the best of you this time." Father Moore paced the floor, hands clasped behind his back. He stopped and looked down at the boy. "It won't be long before you're a grown man, Billy. By that time I hope you will be thinking with your head instead of your fists. They all say you are a natural ballplayer, one of the best. Don't ruin your chances — and your life."

Billy looked up and grinned at Father Moore. "I promise you I'll try, Father. It'll be quite a job for a hotheaded Dago, though." He got up, his face sober. "I don't think they got me mad because they made fun of my face. I think it was because — well, they all seem to have it better than me. They have nice clothes, live in nice houses — and I guess I thought they had no right to bear down on a kid from —— "

The priest nodded. He laid a hand on Billy's shoulder. "I understand, son. While you're trying to keep your promise to me, remember, prayers will help you more than you know."

When Billy left, Father Moore leaned back in his chair, admitting to himself that the boy should not be classed as a sinner, considering his background. God, he was quite certain, would have lots of patience with Billy Martin.

Walking aimlessly in the direction of the docks, Billy became moody and resentful again, even considered the idea of running away from home. He relived the stories Nona told him about a grandfather who used to go away on fishing boats for six months at a time, to China, Alaska, almost everywhere, and come back with a fortune, maybe as much as three hundred dollars. Six blocks from home he came to a sandlot where a bunch of younger kids were playing ball. Baseball fever was stronger in him than wanderlust and he made his way back home.

"There are those books on the table, Bellino," Nona said when he came into the house. "They maybe told you you can't play ball, but they did not say you shouldn't study. To go anywhere you got to have brains. Don't forget that."

Billy was about to put up an argument but changed his mind. He was in his early teens but Nona could still handle him.

For the next three weeks Billy hung around the high school practice field, enviously watching the players work out. He squirmed inwardly as he watched the new shortstop playing his position. The kid couldn't go to his left and his throwing was anything but accurate. He itched to show him how shortstop should be played, but he knew the coach would take a dim view of such a move. Even at sixteen, Billy Martin was a perfectionist on the diamond. If he couldn't be one of the best, then he did not want to play at all. Being the best truck driver or bricklayer was better than being just a fair ballplayer.

He watched the remainder of Berkeley High's home games from the stands, and his shrill voice was heard above all the others. He did his best to root the team into the city championship. The City League fans had forgotten the last game he had played, but they loved to hear him needle the opposing players and shout encouragement to his old teammates. He talked to some of the fans he had once fought and laughed with them. He could never nurse a grudge. Despite moods that came close to being black, he could not keep down the gaiety that always stirred inside him.

The high school textbooks were tougher than all the curved ball pitchers he had ever met. If Columbus had discovered a hard-hitting outfielder instead of America, Billy certainly would have remembered the date. If mathematical problems had been confined to figuring out fielding and batting averages, he would have graduated with honors. His real education involved one subject — baseball. He was certain it would pay off.

After graduation Billy got himself a job in a steel mill as a laborer. He was five feet, five inches tall and weighed only one hundred and twenty-five pounds, but he had unusually strong shoulders and big arms. Older and bigger workmen at the mill lost little time in testing his caliber. When Billy had thoroughly convinced them that he hit like a middleweight, they left him alone. He worked long hours and took all his pay home. Week ends found him at James Kenney Playfield, a well-kept municipal baseball diamond only one block from his home.

To most of the men and boys in the neighborhood the week-end games were their only excuse for existence. Players from thirteen to thirty came there to choose up sides. There were big-leaguers and minor-leaguers there, as well as semipros. The rivalry was bitter, with no quarter asked or given.

The first afternoon Billy showed up with his tattered glove and twenty-five-cent cap, he found a game just getting under way. Walking boldly up to a group of players, he asked who the captain was.

"Hey, it's Billy Martin!" someone shouted above the pregame racket. "The kid who nearly wrecked the high school league." And then an older man, wearing a uniform with TUCSON in faded letters across his chest, stepped in front of Billy. "I've got a full team, kid," he said. "But stick around in case somebody breaks a leg."

He laughed. "You sure got a nose to smell out a ground ball."

Billy's eyes grew hot. "And you've got feet you should hire out to stamp out grass fires," he retorted.

The older man's jaw muscles bulged and he seemed on the verge of chasing Billy off the field. Suddenly his weathered face broke into a wide grin. "Sit down," he said. "What's your name?"

"Martin."

"You look like it should be Garibaldi or something. Well, don't get in the way."

It was a rough game, with Billy watching impatiently from the sidelines. When the shortstop playing for the Blues made his third error and let a run score in the bottom of the fifth, he could stand it no longer. As the Blues came in to bat, he approached the captain and first baseman. "Look, the Grays are in front, five-to-three. Let me in there. I can play shortstop better with boxing gloves on!"

"What can I lose?" the captain snapped. "Eddie is up this inning. I'll let you take his cut."

The lead-off batter crowded the plate and got knocked down, the ball bouncing off his shoulder and rolling close to the wooden stands. He got up, growled at the Grays' pitcher, and strolled to first.

"Okay, kid," the captain said to Billy. "Grab a stick and get up there. Get on any way you can."

Billy walked up to the plate amid a verbal shelling from the week-end crowd. Compared to this reception, the ribbing he had taken in high school had been sweet and mild.

The first pitch came straight at Billy's head and down he went. Getting up slowly, he banged the dirt out of his clothes. He felt like going after the pitcher, then thought of Nona and Father Moore. He grinned and yelled out toward the mound, "You could throw it faster underhand, Buster."

The pitcher brushed him back again, then went to work on him seriously. He finally threw a curve that hung and Billy nailed it. The ball hit less than a foot inside the third sack, going out into deep left, and Billy was on third when the long throw-in reached the infielder. He came in a moment later on a fielder's choice and the score was tied. In the eighth he made his second hit, driving in the run that put the Blues in front. His sparkling defensive play had the crowd solidly on his side. When it was over, older players, many of whom had played in organized ball, agreed that they had seen a big-league prospect that just could not miss. One of them said, "Augie Galan should get a look at that skinny kid."

"He'll have to be held down, though," was another's observation. "His temper is as short as a gopher's tail. He'll fight at the drop of a hat." The player grinned. "But, come to think of it, Frankie Frisch and Johnny Evers were no doves of peace."

Chapter IV

BILLY MARTIN's meeting with Augie Galan was one of the turning points of his life. Galan had played both the infield and the outfield for the Chicago Cubs for sixteen years. Now he was supervisor of the James Kenney Playfield sandlotters. After watching the little shortstop play one afternoon, he knew a star was in the making, and sought Billy out. The youngster from Seventh Street was struck with awe when he found himself in the veteran's presence. It was his first contact with greatness, and when he shook Augie's hand the words he groped for would not come.

"You looked real good out there, kid," Galan told him. "You cover a lot of territory. But they tell me you have quite a temper."

"I've never run away from a fight, Mr. Galan, if that's what they mean. They have to come in at me high and knock me over only once. After that they better watch out for their teeth!"

Augie studied Billy's somber face for a few moments, then grinned. He knew ballplayers. He knew men. He sensed that this boy was governed by inward pressure, not ill nature. There was a lot of the clown in this Billy

37

Martin, a lot of laughter that had been held in check by the rigors of adversity. He had thoroughly checked the boy's background and marveled that he was not more psychologically scarred.

"We have a good team representing James Kenney Playfield," he said. "I think you belong on it. You still have many things to learn, but you have lots of time. We'll try and make a big-league ballplayer out of you."

"Thanks, Mr. Galan," Billy said. "That's all I ever wanted to be."

"It's no piece of cake, Billy. Even if you make a Class C club, you'll live pretty low on the hog. There'll be long rides in busses and hash-house chow. You'll play on bumpy fields and get eaten up by gnats. You'll sleep in cheap hotels and boardinghouses."

"Maybe I've known worse, Mr. Galan." Billy tossed his battered glove up and down in his right hand and grinned at the former big-leaguer for the first time. "Whatever you say it is, it's worth it."

"All right, be out here on Sunday," Augie said. "I'll put you in the line-up."

Billy was still walking on clouds when he arrived home late that afternoon. He tried to tell Nona who Augie Galan was, what a great ballplayer he had been; but there had only been two great men in the game as far as she was concerned: the Bambino and Tony Lazzeri. His stepfather did not have to be told. "You're a lucky kid, Billy," Jack Downey said. "There isn't much Galan doesn't know about the game. You do what he tells you and don't talk back — remember that."

Work in the steel mill built up Billy's shoulders and strengthened his powerful legs. His hard-bitten fellow workers threw in a course of self-control free of charge, and soon the remarks about his big nose and prominent ears were rolling off him like water off the backs of the ducks that flew over Point Isabelle. He was being tempered along with the steel.

Under Galan and the experienced players who gravitated toward James Kenny Playfield on week ends, Billy learned the finer points of infield play. Even in those days he was the spark, the holler guy. Nona told him once that a friend of hers had heard him all the way to the docks.

"I've got a new gag, Nona," Billy confided, chuckling. "You don't have to fight some guys — just give them a real tough look when you pass them. You know, under the eyebrows. It makes them jump. Sure, I holler. You have to let them all know you're around. Father Moore said never to hide your light under a bushel."

His grandmother looked perplexed. "A bushel of what, Bellino?" . . .

Billy Martin's play with the sandlot team soon drew wide attention, and one day Augie brought Red Adams, trainer for the Oakland Acorns, to look him over. Adams managed the Junior Oaks, a semipro team that played ball in Oakland's Pacific Coast League park. It was a training outfit for the Oakland club owned by Brick Laws.

Adams watched Billy play shortstop against a team

from Piedmont, and when the little Italian stretched a single into what seemed an impossible double, he said to Galan, "He's got the aggressiveness it takes — *that* I freely admit."

"He was born with it, Red, believe me," Augie said. "If he hadn't had it in his neighborhood, he'd be dead by now."

Adams watched Billy's every move as the game progressed. A lightning-fast double play started by Billy brought him off his seat. He gasped when the shortstop ran far out into left to catch a fly ball that seemed beyond any fielder's reach. In the ninth he saw Billy slide into second and kick the ball out of the opposing second sacker's glove. When Billy scored later on a single by the Playfield's hard-hitting first baseman, he turned to Galan: "I want him for the Junior Oaks, Augie. Four years at the most, I'd guess, before that kid reaches the big leagues."

"I won't bet against you on that point," Galan said. "I've never seen a kid with more team spirit, or one who loves to play ball like he does."

After the game Augie turned Billy over to Red Adams. "This is a step up, Billy," he said. "Keep your nose clean now. Keep learning."

Billy rubbed his outsized nose with a thumb knuckle and grinned. "A pretty large order, huh?"

He played sparkling, heads-up ball for the Junior Oaks, and his reputation grew. Brick Laws got a good look at him one Sunday afternoon and more than liked what he saw. Billy got word of Laws' being in the stands just after his team took the field in the top of the sixth inning. "It'll be my luck to boot one this time," he said to the third baseman. But he was surprised to discover he had no jitters. He simply felt a great confidence and was determined to make an impression on Laws. He jumped around and yelled at the pitcher. He plucked an imaginary pebble off the skin part of the infield, then hollered some more.

The Junior Oaks hurler was tiring, and walked the first two men to face him. When a heavy hitter moved in, Billy ran to the mound. The spectators all over the park heard what he said: "Stick in there, boy! Bow your neck and get the ball over. We'll take care of the rest."

The power hitter crossed up the Oaks. He shortened up and bunted and was out by a step at first. The tying runs were now on second and third, and the Oaks infield moved in to cut off a run at the plate. Billy yelled words of encouragement at the pitcher as the next hitter came up to bat. The ball blazed in and the batter swung. It looked like a sure hit, but the Oaks shortstop leaped high and caught it in the webbing of his glove. He threw to third and the inning was over.

In the field box, Red Adams glanced at Brick Laws. "Well, what do you think?" he asked.

"I want you to bring that kid to my office tomorrow, Red."

Driving through Oakland's teeming traffic on Monday, Red Adams advised Billy, "Don't say anything to rile him. Just sit tight and listen to Laws because this could really be the turning point."

"What in the world could I say, Red? I'll be too scared to do anything but listen."

"Take any offer. Right now the money isn't as important as getting your foot in the big door."

Half an hour later, however, Red Adams experienced a few bad moments. Looking steadily at Billy, Brick Laws said, "I'll be very frank with you, Martin. We not only want to know what kind of a ballplayer we're hiring, we also want to know what kind of a man he is. I've checked your background carefully, and for your own good I must urge you to break off completely from that tough Seventh Street crowd over in Berkeley. They're rowdies; they consider themselves underprivileged and want to fight the world."

Billy's dark eyes threw sparks. He leaned forward in his chair, his hands balling into fists. Red Adams groaned inwardly and sucked in his breath.

"If that's what you want me to do, Mr. Laws," Billy said steadily, "I don't want to play ball for you. I'll quit first. They're my friends over there and I won't turn my back on them."

Red Adams was about to say something when Laws spoke. The trace of a smile played around the corners of his mouth for an instant. " Perhaps I shouldn't have put it so bluntly, Billy. When you're in organized ball, son, you can't afford to mix with the wrong people. I'll withdraw the stipulation."

"They're my people." The shortstop was emphatic. "They always will be."

"Loyalty in a man is a good quality," Brick Laws

said. "Now, about a contract, Martin. How does two hundred dollars a month sound?" His glance brushed the clothes Billy wore. "And three hundred dollars for a wardrobe thrown in."

Billy was certain he was dreaming. In a few moments he would hear Nona calling for him to get out of bed, that he was already late for work at the mill. He had never had more than twenty dollars in his pocket in his whole life. He turned his eyes toward Red Adams, who said, "It's a good offer, Billy."

Brick Laws handed the bewildered shortstop a pen and pushed some papers toward him. "Sign your full name."

Billy got closer to the desk and banged his knee against it. He winced a little but felt no pain. The sensation assured him that this was not a dream but real. Taking the pen from Laws, he started to write, then held up. Red Adams squirmed in his chair.

Full name? Alfred Manuel Martin? Oh no! Billy remembered the many fights he'd had on Seventh Street. He signed the contract and Laws picked it up, studying it. "*Billy* Martin. That's your legal name?"

"It is." There was a trace of an edge in Billy's voice. "What's wrong with it?"

Brick Laws smiled and held out his hand. "Lots of luck," he said. "I'm certain we made a good investment. Just wait a few minutes and I'll have a check made out to you."

"I'll wait all day," Billy said.

When he left the building Billy was the property of

the Oakland ball club and he had a check for three
hundred dollars in his pocket. Outside the world had
become transformed, the sidewalks felt like foam rub-
ber under his feet. Oakland had suddenly become as
enchanting as Disneyland. As a thought suddenly
struck him, he laughed out loud. "Remember that day
last year, Red? The day I told Casey Stengel I'd be
playing ball for him someday? Wait until he hears
the news!"

"I've got a hunch he already knows, Billy. But you
won't be playing for him right away, you know. The
Oak front office will farm you out somewhere."

"But not for long."

Red Adams sensed the excitement, the overanxiety
in the boy walking beside him. He wished Billy had
one important thing — steadiness. He knew the grief
ballplayers run into, that only one bright prospect out
of four is equal to the test. "Take it slow and easy,
Billy," he advised. "Don't be too impatient and you'll
hit the top."

"What's that saying, Red? 'Don't put off until tomorrow what you can do today.' It makes sense."

"And 'haste makes waste,'" the trainer countered.

"Looks like we ended in a tie." Billy laughed as he
stepped into Adams' parked car.

He burst into the frame house on Seventh Street just
as the family was about to sit down for the noonday
meal. He picked his beloved Nona right off the floor
and hugged her, sat her in a chair, and held the three-
hundred-dollar check in front of her eyes. Then he

pressed it into one of her work-hardened hands. "I'm a real pro, Nona," he shouted. "Two hundred dollars every month with the Oaks. This check is to buy all the clothes I need. There's enough for new dresses for you and Mama. A shotgun for Jack, too. For Joanie I'll —— "

The family swarmed around him; never had there been such excitement in the household. With tears in her eyes Nona said, "So haven't I always said you would be a ballplayer, Bellino? Only now you believe me, no?"

Billy turned to his stepfather. "You go and buy something special for supper. Here's some money. And get yourself a big cigar, Jack." He picked up his mother and kissed her. "No more hand-me-downs for the Martins."

Supper was a real celebration. "From now on," Billy said, "you'll all have ice cream every day. When I get to the Yankees I'll buy you a washing machine, Mama. I'll —— "

"Whoa, Billy. Slow down!" his stepfather cautioned. "You're aiming pretty high. The Yankees —— !"

"And who are these Yankee paisans that are too good for my Bellino?" Nona shouted indignantly. "You wait and see, Jack Downey. Only the best for my Bellino."

Billy took a walk that afternoon and soon learned that word of his good fortune had spread all over the neighborhood. People leaned out of windows and called to him. Many who stopped him on the street had felt the sting in his fists. Now everything was forgotten. They took pride in knowing this Italian boy from the slums.

Father Moore was greatly pleased. "It is a most wonderful thing that has happened," he beamed. "To all boys here, not only you. It shows others that a humble beginning is not a hopeless thing, that better things are within the reach of everyone." When he walked away he said softly, "God be with you, Billy Martin."

That night in his room, Billy picked up his old infielder's glove and turned it over and over in his hands. He knew he'd never have another he would like as well, not if it cost him a hundred dollars.

Chapter V

OAKLAND SENT BILLY MARTIN to Idaho Falls in the Pioneer League. There they made a third baseman out of him and his troubles began. Very little money was spent on keeping the playing fields in shape so that the players almost expected gophers to pop out of the ground at any time and spoil a double play or run off with the baseball. Billy played thirty-two games in 1946 and made sixteen errors. He had a terrible time making the throw from third. Although his arm was strong, his throws to first were erratic. Most of the time the ball curved.

One day Jim Stanton, who alternated at first base with Walt Bricker, told Billy, "Look, kid, if I wanted to catch curves, I'd have learned to be a catcher. And it's against the rules to put a first baseman's mitt on the end of a pole."

Billy knew his wild throws were caused by his slowness in getting the ball out of his glove when he'd picked up a swinging bunt or raced in to meet a slow-hit ground ball. He spent hours practicing grabbing the ball out of his glove with two fingers, aiming his throw, coming in at full speed to get the ball in his bare

47

hand, and learning to throw accurately off balance. His determination paid off and he became a solid infielder before he left the Pioneer League.

Only eighteen years old, he had not completely overcome his homesickness. Most of the players had long since cast their first votes. A lot of them had steady girl friends; but Billy was more afraid of girls than getting knocked down by a fast ball. To his chagrin, the older players would not allow him to follow them into places selling anything stronger than root beer.

Despite his loneliness he never lost his sense of humor. He was a great mimic and his take-offs on some of the players and umpires around the league kept his teammates roaring with laughter. They needed his sparkling wit and gaiety, especially during the long, tedious bus rides. They enjoyed his joshing during meals, for the food was most unappetizing even for a kid brought up on Berkeley's Seventh Street. There were two players on the Idaho Falls team who had been in the major leagues for a short time. They played in the present but lived mostly in the past; listening to their talk, Billy promised himself that once he got to the big leagues he would stay there.

He was no great ball of fire with Idaho Falls. In his thirty-two games, he hit only .254, but there was something about the youngster from California that made the fans forget about batting and fielding averages. His supreme confidence in himself and his fiery temperament told them that he would not be long in bush-league baseball.

In 1947 the Oakland front office sent him to Phoenix in the Arizona-Texas League, and there he gave thanks for the first time in his life that he had been born near the docks of San Francisco Bay. The team was called the Junior Gas House Gang and was managed by a rough-and-ready man named Arkie Biggs, who played second base. Their battle cry was, "Knock 'em down!" and they made the lives of the umpires miserable. Their antics delighted the fans, however. One gag was to build a fire in front of the dugout with the temperature a hundred in the shade and warm their hands over it.

Billy found himself in his element. When Biggs met him for the first time, the manager eyed him up and down and shook his head. "Looks like they steal 'em out of cradles in Oakland. Look, we can't afford a bat boy. Man, this bunch will chase you out of town."

Several of the Phoenix players moved in close, gleams in their eyes. Billy glared at them, his legs wide apart, his fists clenched. "They're welcome to try it right now, Mr. Biggs," he said. "They don't look so tough!"

Biggs laughed. Sudden respect for the newcomer came into his eyes. "All right, you guys," he yelled at his players. "Go on out there and work out — and no loafing!"

The team traveled great distances — to El Paso, Tucson, Júarez, and Bisbee. The players were crammed into two station wagons, with their gear loaded into trailers bouncing along behind. The unmarried men lived in a Quonset hut inside the ball park, and Billy soon found out that a fair amount of fistic talent was needed if a guy wished to retain possession of even a tube of toothpaste. Two of the players quickly learned not to tangle with him.

Billy played third base that year and proceeded to prove that Augie Galan's judgment of him had been correct. Every pitcher in the Arizona-Texas League became his "cousin" and as a glove man he covered an amazing amount of territory. His aggressiveness and continuous chatter kept the other players hustling. When his temper erupted on or off the field even Biggs was careful with his words. His reputation grew, and the crowds all over the circuit grew along with it.

The others players thoroughly hated Billy at first, but his contagious personality was impossible to resist. They found him an entertaining, generous fellow, even began to admire his ego that at first had rubbed them raw. His talkativeness and love for a gag made the long road trips bearable.

On the way back to Phoenix one day, the station wagons stopped at a farm to allow the players to stretch their legs. When Billy got out of the car, his dark eyes widened at the sight of a flock of fat turkeys on the other side of a fence. He turned to pitcher Don Cantrell, and grinned broadly. "Keep Arkie busy. I'm gettin' us one of those birds."

"It'll murder you, Billy," Cantrell protested. "It'll claw your ears off!"

Getting over the fence in a hurry, Billy almost immediately found himself in a lively tussle with a big gobbler. He was covered with scratches and his slacks were ripped before he had subdued it. Wrapping the big bird in his uniform, he carried it back to the station wagon.

Nearly a mile away from the farm, the turkey got his head loose and started to gobble. "What was that?" Arkie yelled back.

"It's that noise in the engine again," Billy said while the other players fought to keep their laughter under wraps.

"I never heard no noise under a hood like that before," Biggs growled.

"Nobody ever saw a jalopy like this one before either," outfielder Don Barclay called out.

The noise came again and Biggs braked the station wagon. There was a beat of wings, followed by a loud squawk, and Arkie swung around in the driver's seat and saw the turkey.

"Take it back!" he yelled. "Martin, you crazy meathead, there's a law against stealing turkeys."

"Look, Arkie," Billy protested, "I'm cut and bleeding. I earned this bird. We could cook it back at the Quonset hut. We're all sick of hamburgers and tough pot roast."

"Turn it loose," Biggs bellowed, "or I'll fine you ten bucks!"

Billy grunted his displeasure but complied. Before he got the turkey through the door, one of its claws nearly took part of Arkie's ear off. "Why didn't you stay in Idaho Falls?" he roared at Billy when the third baseman finally let the bird loose.

"If I had, you'd still be in fifth place," Billy said.

"You fresh busher!" Biggs fumed and stepped on the gas.

"Looks like you fowled out, Billy!" Pete Hughes, the right fielder, laughed.

Phoenix looked like a cinch for the pennant until the night they went to Bisbee to play under the lights. Bisbee had a pugnacious catcher whom Billy Martin was to meet and always remember later in his career. His name was Clint Courtney. The game was hardly an hour old when Courtney spiked Arkie Biggs as he slid into second base. The manager's legs were cut to the bone and he had to be helped off the field.

When the umpires finally restored order, Billy took over at second base, a position strange to him. Courtney, standing on the bag, grinned at him. Billy had watched the last play closely and knew the spiking had been deliberate. He was still hot under the collar and glared at Courtney. "Someday," he promised, "a guy will shove the ball down your throat!"

"Maybe I'll be coming this way in a hurry again tonight, kid. You try it."

"I just might," Billy said and moved into his unfamiliar position. The palms of his hands were moist and his legs shook a little. Could he make the pivot if the double-play situation arose? And if he could, would he be able to get the ball to first before the base runner bowled him over? He was not long in finding out.

Playing second base proved even rougher than Billy imagined. He made fifty-five errors. Phoenix fans claimed that the spiking of Arkie Biggs cost them the pennant; they placed none of the blame on Billy Martin. In one hundred and thirty games he batted .392, and his two hundred and thirty hits set an Arizona-Texas League record. He drove in one hundred and seventy-four runs and stole thirty-one bases.

Casey Stengel called him back to Oakland that year. The team was loaded with former major leaguers, fast company for a rookie. Billy played both second and third base, hitting only .226. He made five errors, and when he emptied his locker in September he could see himself back with Phoenix again, taking those long hauls to El Paso and Júarez, and sweating out the nights in a Quonset hut. When he was ready to leave the clubhouse for home, he sought out the Oakland manager. "Casey," he said, "I was real bad, wasn't I?"

"Well, not good," Stengel said. "But you'll learn, Billy. A little buck fever, let's call it. Even birds have to learn to fly. I kind of figure you in my plans for next year, so don't go jumping in the bay."

"Thanks, Case." Billy's ego flickered brightly once more and his spirits soared. He put on a new sports coat, flicked an imaginary spot of dust from his sleeve, and checked himself in the mirror. Vince DiMaggio, now in the twilight of his career, came by. "Pretty snappy," he complimented. "Say, drop in at Fisherman's Wharf someday, Billy. Everything'll be on the house. You ought to get to really know Joe. You could be playing with him someday."

"Say, wouldn't that be something!"

"You'll have to hurry, though, kid. Joe is no spring chicken," Vince laughed. When he had gone, Billy sat down and wondered how many dreams could come true. Playing in the same line-up with the Yankee Clipper! That was the very top.

At Oakland in 1948 he was a youngster in the midst of such veteran campaigners as Harry "Cookie" Lavagetto, Nick Etten, Maurice Van Robays, and George Metkovitch. This was the acid test but he held his own, both at shortstop and second base, despite the merciless riding given him by the bench jockeys of the Pacific Coast League. Even his own teammates worked him over at the start of the season, but he held onto his temper and self-assurance, rapidly proving to all concerned that he was big-league material.

The other players never ceased to wonder how Billy got away with the way he talked to Stengel. One day Casey halted a workout and walked over to Billy. "Look, kid, you ain't just out there jitterbugging," he said. "Let me show you how to make that double play properly."

"If you can't do it, Case, don't knock it. My way is good enough," Billy yelled back.

They expected Stengel to thumb Billy to the clubhouse and sit him down for a week, but Casey just turned around and walked away, a hand up over his face to hide a grin.

Words Billy generally ignored, but he resented unnecessary roughness on the part of opposing players.

He always struck back, and some of the battles in which he was involved nearly cut his baseball career short. One night he was badly spiked and was carried into the dressing room. He yelled at his teammates to turn him loose. "I'm going after that guy! Let me go!"

They brought a doctor out of the stands, and four husky players held him down while his cuts were sewed up. Nick Etten said, "You won't be back for two weeks."

"I'll take bets on that," Billy muttered through his pain.

Later in the season he tangled with Lou Stringer in Hollywood, setting off one of the greatest free-for-alls ever seen on the Coast. Even Casey Stengel moved in and did some swinging. Billy came out of the melee with a sore knee and a stiff neck that side-lined him for a while. But he got back into the line-up and helped Oakland win its first pennant in twenty-one years. He hit .277 that year and turned in a respectable .966 fielding average.

He played in one hundred and seventy-two games for Oakland in 1949 and hit .286. He fielded .962. It was the year the New York Yankees brought Casey Stengel up to manage the Bombers and turned the Oakland club over to Charlie Dressen. There were tears in Billy's eyes when he shook hands with Old Case and wished him luck. "I'll be seeing you, Billy, which won't be too long," Stengel said. "And listen, don't get in no more fights."

Several weeks later Billy was playing in a night game at Oakland when an advertising blimp sailed over the diamond. Hamrick at shortstop yelled, "Look, Billy!" but his voice was drowned out by the sudden roar from the crowd. At the plate the batter moved out of the box and looked skyward. Then Billy looked up and saw the lighted letters on the blimp spelling out the late news:

BILLY MARTIN SOLD TO THE YANKEES

He wondered if his eyes were playing tricks on him. But then he heard a voice from somewhere in the in-field. "You lucky stiff, you!"

Billy banged a fist into his glove and hollered at the Oaks pitcher. He felt ten feet tall. He was a Yankee. The message had come from high above. He looked up into the lights, his eyes searching far beyond them. Once more he heard a voice saying, "Always remember to say your prayers, Bellino. Somebody will listen, you will find out."

His grandmother had passed away in 1946 and had taken a big part of Billy's heart with her. She would know he had made it, he thought as a hard-hit ball came scorching to his left. He raced over, dug it out of the dirt, and fired to first. An ache formed a lump in his throat. "In spirit," Father Dennis Moore had said, "Nona will always be with you, Billy."

In the dressing room after the game the Oaks gave Billy a celebration. When the excitement had cooled, a player asked, "What are you getting for signing? They say Jackie Jensen got over sixty grand."

"I don't know, but they'll sure pay me what I'm worth," Billy said.

"Nobody could live on it," Van Robays needled. "Sure, we get a real ball club and then they raid us. Without Jensen they expect us to win a pennant. Already the Yanks have DiMag and Henrich, but —— "

"And that Dago, Martin, don't forget," Nick Etten quipped. "They must be desperate in New York."

Billy grinned as he laced his street shoes. Casey Stengel would know what he was worth. The Yankee front office would pay it. Sure, Jensen had been more than a .300 hitter for Oakland, but heavy hitting alone did not make a ball club. Without a tight infield it would go nowhere.

When Billy learned the details of the deal, he was fighting mad. Oakland was paying him nine thousand dollars, but the Yankees were offering him only the minimum of seventy-five hundred. He knew that the scouts had been high on him weeks ago and had pinned a fifty-thousand-dollar price tag on him. Now he was told that it was Jackie Jensen the Yanks had really wanted and he had merely been thrown in as part of the purchase price.

"Just a throw-in, huh?" he yelled at Brick Laws. "I've got a good mind to quit!"

"Look, Billy, there was a good price on you until you got hurt in that brawl involving Lou Stringer. They know about that bad knee you got out of it. Keep your head. You've got a chance to show the Yankees what you're really worth. When you do they'll up your contract."

"Okay," Billy gave in, his dark eyes bright with determination. "I'll show them. I'll stay up there longer than Jensen. I'll bet on that."

Laws shook his head. "A man with half a brain never bets against Billy Martin," he thought, and held out his hand. "Good luck, Billy. I know you'll become one of the best."

Charlie Dressen talked to him before he left Oakland. "Bear this in mind, Billy. You're a big name out here, but you'll be just a green busher when you walk into Yankee Stadium. Don't pop off there and show your press clippings. The Yankees are the best in the business, and you'll have to prove you belong in their company. They'll resent your trying to take a job away from one of the veterans, but they'll also give you every chance to prove you can do it. Just watch that temper of yours, Billy, and keep your fists in your pocket. All the other teams in that league gun for the Yanks and pull no punches. They'll gun for you, too."

"Thanks," Billy said. "I'll remember."

When he had gone, Dressen turned to one of the Oakland players. "You know something, I didn't scare him a bit." He chuckled and headed for his office. "I bet he'll even sass Frankie Crosetti, and stow his stuff in DiMag's locker."

Chapter VI

WHEN BILLY walked into the lobby of the Hotel Soreno in St. Petersburg early in the spring of 1950, he was sure he recognized several Yankee players lounging around: Rizzuto, Henrich, Collins, and Reynolds. He felt their eyes on him when he registered at the desk. On his way from Berkeley he kept telling himself there was nothing to be scared about. He would not bow and scrape to these famous players.

Oh, they had a right to be proud. They had to have something extra, else they never would have become Yankees. He was positive he had it too. That was why he was here. Five minutes later he was talking with Casey Stengel in the manager's suite. Stengel said, "You look skinnier than ever, Billy, but I'm glad you're here. Have you met any of the others?"

"I saw some down in the lobby," Billy said, and looked the manager straight in the eye. "Something tells me you've been talking to them about me."

"Maybe I told them a story or two," Casey said, grinning. "Maybe I told them you were the kind of fella we need in this ball club."

Billy drummed his fingers against the arm of his

59

chair. His hands were never still. "They know I came here to take somebody's job away, Case, not to sit on the bench. Second, third, or shortstop is all right with me."

"Still in a big hurry," Stengel said. "We're pretty solid in the infield, Billy. You just keep your shirt on and maybe someday —— "

Billy interrupted him with a short laugh. "I had a rough time getting this far, Case. I put in a lot of hours on the sandlots and the minors, and I figure on staying here."

"You go get some rest and then feed yourself, Billy," Stengel said. "I'm glad to see you're as fresh as ever."

Billy's face was a little sober when he left Stengel. If determination and the will to succeed were mistaken for brashness, it was all right with him. All he had ever wanted was a chance to prove he belonged, and he would battle the whole Yankee team, one by one, if he had to.

The sunny smile came back to his face when he reached his room. He could see the blue waters of the Gulf of Mexico from the window; the water craft spotting it reminded him that he had never had the time or money for much recreation. It was time he got his share. He threw his shoulders back and smiled broadly as he recalled what the clerk downstairs had said to a man who was checking in ahead of him. Sorry, but he could not accommodate him without a reservation. The man had looked like a broker or a banker. But there had been a room ready for Billy Martin. A Yankee player was sure somebody.

He met Stengel's Bombers in the clubhouse the next afternoon and felt awe in their presence in spite of himself. But he did not let them know it. Johnny Lindell, the big outfielder, made it plain that Billy's debut would be rough in spots. "We've heard a lot about you, Martin," he said. He grinned at several other players standing by, then shook his head. "The terror of the coast league. Say, kid, what do you weigh soaking wet?"

"I'm heavier than I look," Billy replied, knowing that his ears were getting red.

"Pack your bags," Cliff Mapes said to Jerry Coleman. "This guy is going to cut your job right from under you."

Billy said, "I'm here to try." He gave Coleman a grin, and the second baseman returned it. That broke a lot of ice.

During the days that followed, the Bombers gave Billy the full treatment they reserved for all rookies, both on and off the field. Often he found himself hitting the dirt to stop wild throws that came his way when he worked out in the infield. They bumped him off-balance when they came close to him, accidentally of course, tempting him to lose his temper and swing his fists. He was more surprised than they were at the way he took the abuse, but one day he realized that it was time he stood his ground and fought back. It began when the Yankees took a serious workout in the cage to sharpen up their batting eyes.

Billy moved in after Rizzuto had taken his swings and felt himself nudged out of the way by Johnny Lindell. "Take your turn when it comes, kid," the outfielder said. "And get yourself a lighter bat."

The other players waited, grinning with anticipation. His Latin temperament flaring up, Billy turned and strode toward Casey Stengel who was talking with Crosetti. "Case, I've taken all I'm going to. If you don't want some cripples in this ball club, let me go up and hit. I don't care how big that Lindell is. I'll —— "

"John," Stengel called out. "Billy Martin is going to take his cuts."

"Why, sure, Case," the outfielder said and came out of the cage. When he stopped to wave the fielders in, a burst of laughter came from the Bombers grouped back of the wire screen.

Billy took his stance at the plate, his feet spread wide, his bat cocked high over his right shoulder. He sent two screaming line drives to the outfield and nearly knocked the batting practice pitcher down with a scorching drive past second. Somehow the bat slipped out of his hand when he took his last swing and it skidded along the ground toward the Yankee dugout, missing a small group of Bombers by less than a foot.

"It was an accident, Case, honest," Billy said to the manager as he walked away from the plate. He knew the other Yankees would never believe it.

As the training season went on, the writers wanted to know why Stengel had brought up this fresh rookie from Oakland when his infield was the strongest in the American League. It had to be for sentimental reasons. Billy read that he was a hot-tempered kid from the Berkeley docks, quick to use his fists, and possessed of the arrogance of a Leo Durocher. Words they put in his mouth which he'd never said caused some resentment among the other players.

One night the journalists ambushed him at the Soreno and tried to get him to talk about his escapades on the coast. "Look, you fellows," he said, a smile on his dark face, "you have to make a living too, or you don't eat. But a lot of the stuff you've been saying about me you might have to eat. I'm just a Dago trying to make the Yankee ball club."

"You can't help but like him," one of the writers said after Billy had gone on his way. "I think he'll be around for a long time."

As the days passed at St. Petersburg, it was plain to everyone concerned that Billy Martin was a skillful glove man who possessed a great fighting spirit and a deep love for the game of baseball. While he sat the bench and watched George Stirnweiss and Jim Brideweser take turns at playing second base, he squirmed with impatience and cooled himself off by raving at Yankee mistakes and loudly approving of their shows of skill. His shrill, high-pitched voice dominated every practice session.

When the real trials against other major league clubs drew near, Billy kept pestering Stengel. "Let me in there, Case. Why did you bring me up? You've got a batboy."

"Just take it easy, Billy. You'll get your chance," Stengel kept saying.

Billy jumped to his feet. Hank Bauer had just been caught at second on a force-out. "Hey, Hank, you worried about dirtying your monkey suit?" he yelled. "That the way the Marines taught you to hit the dirt?"

The other Yankees stared at him, still not fully accustomed to his impudence, his apparent disregard of big Yankee reputations. They kept wondering at Stengel, who seemed to thoroughly enjoy the brat's antics and ceaseless chatter; but they had to admit that something had happened to the ball club. The players, even at this time of year, were making that extra bit of effort. They were fired up this year weeks ahead of time.

March 11, 1950, was a red-letter day in Billy's life. Stengel announced to the writers that Billy Martin would play short for the Yankees against the St. Louis Cardinals. He told Billy, "Make me look good today, kid. Show them why you're here."

"We'll run them out of the park," Billy said.

The Cards came in with players like Enos Slaughter, Stan Musial, Marty Marion, Garagiola, and Schoendienst. They were given a big chance to win the 1950 National League pennant. When the game began and Walker came up to lead off for the Cards, Billy Johnson, playing third for Stengel, glanced over at the rookie from Berkeley who was already yelling defiance at the St. Louis bench, and heckling the man at the plate.

"Look out they don't stomp you, Martin," Johnson yelled at the shortstop.

Sanford started for the Yankees and held the Cardinals in check. The Yankees pounded four St. Louis pitchers. None of them could get Billy out. He walked his first two times up, and then in the fifth, after Joe

DiMaggio and Billy Johnson had singled, he knelt in the batting circle and watched Lindell swing against Yuhas the St. Louis pitcher. The outfielder flied out, and Billy walked to the plate with the jockeying from the Cards' bench filling his ears.

He kept remembering what Augie Galan had told him: "Get rabbit ears and you won't last long." He got set and looked down at the third base coach. Hit away, he was told. He let one go by that was a little inside, and the umpire called it a strike. He got some dirt on his hands, then took his wide stance again. He liked the next pitch and swung hard. The ball went into short left for a single and Joe DiMaggio raced home.

In the sixth he cut down a Cardinal rally with a stop of a hard-hit ball by Marion, and turned it into a double play. It was only one of several sparkling plays that brought smiles to Stengel's weather-beaten face.

The Yankees kept hammering. Billy drove in another run in the seventh and wound up with a perfect day at bat, two walks and two hits. The Bombers won, 15-4.

In the dressing room the Yankees paid the rookie little attention. They had seen bush leaguers shine brightly before and then fade. Anyway, this Martin was cocky enough and there was no sense in making him worse. But Billy felt wonderful under the shower. He knew he could keep going. He would stay with the Yankees.

That day Rud Rennie, of the New York *Herald Tribune,* wrote, "Martin, a young infielder from Oakland, did a nice job at shortstop. He covers a lot of ground and has sure hands, gets the ball away fast. He made two hits and walked twice."

He kept up his great playing against the Red Sox and the Senators, and was slowly but surely establishing himself as a holler guy, a little buzzing wasp that stung the veterans to do their very best. The Yankees enjoyed his sharp wit and admired his talents, but often felt the urge to murder him. After one game with the Senators, Joe Page, Stengel's ace relief pitcher, stormed into the manager's office.

"You know, Case?" Page yelled, "That busher came to the mound and told me what to pitch! Telling *me* what to throw! What's he got on you, Case? How does he get away with it?"

"That's a real good question, fella," Stengel said and walked away, chuckling.

Billy met an old friend when the Yanks played the Red Sox at Sarasota. The score was tied in the last of the eleventh, 6-6, when Billy Goodman, leading off for Boston, doubled off Hood, Stengel's rookie pitcher. Lou Stringer, up next, waited Hood out and drew a walk. Billy looked across the diamond at Stringer, who took his lead off first. The glances of the two ex-coast league players met. Stringer remembered and gave Billy a smile.

Silvera suddenly fired to second when Goodman took too long a lead. Caught off, Goodman raced toward third and was run down. Stringer took second on the play, and Billy looked over at him. "Sure, we had quite a mixup at Hollywood," he said, laughing. "I still feel it, Lou."

"Think you'll stay up here, Billy?"

"If an old wreck like you can," Billy said and laughed loudly.

"I believe it now," Stringer said. "You never bear a grudge."

"Say, who won that fight anyhow?" Billy said and moved away.

The Bombers soon gave up trying to put Billy in what they considered was his proper place, and most of them had to admit that they had been won over by his infectious grin and fighting spirit. They showed him in no way, however, what their true feelings were. He still did not feel that he really belonged — not until the afternoon when, slumped in a chair in the lobby of the hotel he was wondering as to his fate when the Yankees would be cut to the twenty-five-player limit. Hearing a voice say, "Kid, let's go eat," he looked up and saw the great Joe DiMaggio looking down at him.

He could hardly believe it: Joe, who had been his idol for many years. Like himself, Joe had come up the hard way from the San Francisco Bay section.

"Huh? You mean —— ?"

"Come on, Billy. We Italians have to stick together," the Yankee Clipper said.

It was the beginning of a close companionship and it broke down what barriers remained between Billy and the other Bombers. It did more than people ever realized to inspire Billy Martin to reach the goal he had set for himself.

Chapter VII

"I'm a little scared, Joe," Billy said to DiMaggio one day when they returned from a fishing trip. "It won't be long before they cut this squad, and Casey has plenty of veteran infielders. I heard George Weiss was against his calling me up anyway."

"Don't cross a bridge until you come to it, Billy. I wish I could tell you your job is safe here, but after all I'm not the front office." DiMaggio eyed Billy closely. "But if you do get sent back, no matter where, you keep playing your head off, the best you know how."

"You can bet I will," Billy said, his dark eyes flashing. "If there is anything I hate, Joe, it's a quitter!"

He proved that statement beyond all doubt a few days later when the Yanks played the New Orleans Pelicans at St. Petersburg. Stengel started Dick Wakefield, one of the highest-priced bonus players in the history of the game, in right field. Detroit had given up on him. From outward appearances he looked like a natural ballplayer. His heart, however, was not deep enough in the game of baseball.

In the eighth Merson, a good hitter for New Orleans,

drove a short, towering fly to right. Billy, at second base for the Yankees, watched Wakefield break late from his position. The man loafed in, and Billy started shouting, "Come on, come on!" Realizing the ball would drop, he raced out into the outfield. He picked the ball up, whirled, and fired it into the infield, then tore after Wakefield.

"You big lazy stiff! You could have caught it in your cap!" Billy raged. "What are you doing in a Yankee uniform?"

The big outfielder glared at him and seemed about to charge, but Billy stood his ground.

Merson, on second, laughed. "This the way they play in the big leagues?" he called out, and Wakefield suddenly walked away.

Billy came back to his position, shaking his head, for there was a player he could not understand. He had always played to win whether the stakes were very big or very small. He angrily kicked up dirt and glared at the New Orleans base runner. "No, they don't play that way in the big leagues," he said. "That's why he won't be around long."

He dismissed Wakefield from his mind a few moments later when the Pelicans' catcher slammed a ball into the hole between first and second. He cut off what seemed a sure hit and threw off-balance to first to nip the runner by a step. He looked out at Wakefield after making the play, thankful for the difference between himself and the bonus player.

The Yankees moved into Brooklyn on April 26th to

play the Dodgers at Ebbets Field, and a big crowd turned out to see the 1950 edition of the Yankees. The fans were to see for the first time the player who was to be a thorn in the side of the famous Bums in the not-so-distant future. Their first impression of him was one of scorn. That scrawny Dago! That was the firebrand from Oakland? Why, if he got in Jackie's way there would be murder!

The Brooklyn players felt his presence in a hurry. Billy hurled defiance at them from the dugout steps, and veterans like Hodges, Furillo, and Campanella were left speechless for a while at the brashness of this Yankee rookie. Once he yelled at Jackie Robinson, "If I was in your league, Fatso, I'd have your job."

The game was played under the lights. Billy drank in the magic of big-league baseball as he warmed up at second base. He had never heard a noisier crowd. All the baseball writers in the country seemed to be crammed into the press box. The great Preacher Roe was warming up for the Dodgers. A lot of Yankee fans had come from across the river and he knew they would be watching him closely to find out just why he rated a Yankee uniform.

It was anybody's game for six innings. Roe and Raschi were pitching in mid-season form. Billy, the first time up against the veteran Brooklyn pitcher, could do nothing against the wide curves that came his way. Neither could Joe DiMaggio or Berra or any of the other heavy hitters. But he had the fans buzzing with his play at second base. He had cut off what seemed sure hits off the bats of Peewee Reese and Gene Hermanski, and once he raced into right for a fly ball off Furillo's big bat and caught it over his shoulder.

"Come on," Stengel yelled as the Yankees came in for their times at bat in the seventh. "Get us some runs."

Billy kept his eyes on Preacher Roe out on the pitching mound. It seemed to him that the veteran had been taking more time between pitches the last couple of innings. Joe DiMaggio led off for the Yanks and caught hold of a pitch and drove it deep into the stands for a home run.

Yogi Berra stepped in. Billy hollered, "Make it two, Yog!" He was off the bench, clapping his hands. But Berra hit weakly to second and was thrown out. Billy Johnson hit a single and the relief pitchers in the Brooklyn bullpen got the word to warm up in a hurry. Johnny Lindell worked the count to two balls and two strikes, then singled to right.

Billy Martin came up to the plate, and a Brooklyn fan yelled, "Two out, Preach!"

The Brooklyn bench tried to rattle the rookie from Oakland. Campy kept talking it up, figuring to unnerve him. Roe made him wait. He fidgeted out on the mound, rubbed the ball up, and took his own time checking the base runners.

"Throw it, Preach," an impatient fan shouted. "He can't hit you with a plank!"

Billy's only concern since he had played in the sandlots was his hitting. Thus far he had not hit a loud foul ball off Roe. But he could always hit when runners were on, he told himself. And then a pitch he liked came streaking in and he swung with all his might. He knew by the crack of the bat that he had hit it solidly. The ball went into the corner in deep left and he reached second before the ball came in to the infield. Billy Johnson crossed the plate.

Standing on second, Billy felt that nothing could stop him now. If he could hit Preacher Roe, he could get his share of hits off the pitchers in the American League. When Roe faced the next hitter, Raschi, Billy danced off second. The Yankee fans roared with delight at the way he bothered the Brooklyn pitcher. They could hear Billy yelling at Raschi.

The Yankee pitcher, never a great hitter, drove one through the infield for a hit and another run scored. A conference was held at the pitching mound, and then Podbeilan was called in from the Brooklyn bullpen. The Dodger fans cheered Roe as he shuffled toward the dugout. Five runs came across for the Yankees before the relief pitcher got the third out.

The Brooklyn batters kept pecking away at Raschi and threatened to even matters in the eighth. With a man on and only one out, Billy raced to his right and stabbed a hard grounder off Eddie Morgan's bat and got the force at second by an eyelash. Raschi looked out at Billy and grinned, then went to work on Don Zimmer and got the side out. He finally walked off the mound with a 6-4 win.

"You did all right, Billy," Casey Stengel said in the

visitors' dressing room, and when the writers moved in he said, "Like I said, that feller won't bust no fences, but when you need that hit —— "

Billy's enthusiasm wore off with the shower. The big test was yet to come. After all, this had only been an exhibition game that did not count in the pennant race, and Preacher Roe had not been really bearing down.

"We'll get that Parnell up in Boston," Berra said. "I hope we can break that Indian sign he has on us."

"And there's that Stobbs," Henrich said. "Don't forget him!"

Billy tried to keep the names of certain pitchers out of his mind. Great hurlers like Bob Lemon, Billy Pierce, and Sid Hudson. They spelled the doom of many an ambitious rookie.

DiMaggio sensed Billy's unease as he took the rookie around New York. He introduced him to Toots Shor's and Danny's Hideaway. Billy told DiMaggio, "They won't take this away from me, Joe. This is the way I want to live. You were right: there's no place like New York."

"Sure, it can be good to you, kid," the Clipper said. "It can also ruin you, depending on the kind of people you pick for your friends. Remember, I won't be around long to keep you out of trouble." He grinned and called for the dinner check, and when Billy glanced at it, he recalled that the Martin family had often lived on half the amount for a full week. On the way to the hotel DiMaggio asked, "You nervous about the opener in Boston, Billy?"

"All I worry about is, will Casey start me, Joe."

"When I broke in, Billy, I don't believe I had half your confidence. And only a little of your determination. I don't see how you can miss."

"I'm not going to, Joe," Billy said. "I promised somebody I wouldn't. Sometime I'll tell you about her."

Fenway Park in Boston was jammed on April 18th. The Red Sox were favored to win the pennant, packing such power as Ted Williams, Bobby Doerr, Junior Stephens, Johnny Pesky, and Dom DiMaggio.

Billy's heart sank when Stengel announced his lineup for the opening game. Jerry Coleman would start at second base, rounding out the strong 1950 infield of Billy Johnson, Rizzuto, and Tommy Henrich. After working out, Billy went to the dugout and watched Mel Parnell warm up. He looked fast. They said he could curve the best hitters to death. Allie Reynolds, the Chief, would work for Casey, so Billy knew Parnell had better be good.

He could not sit still. He moved around, hollering at the Yankee players, ribbing the Red Sox who came close to the dugout. "Look out for that Birdie Tebbets," Stengel said to him. "He'll talk even you off your feet, Billy."

Soon it was game time, and Billy yelled encouragement to Phil Rizzuto, who was to lead off for the Bombers. The crowd came to life when Parnell turned loose his first pitch and slipped it past the Scooter for a strike. The home fans soon got much more to cheer about. Boston's hitters found the range and knocked

Reynolds out of the box. They kept hitting when Sanford came in. Casey Stengel walked up and down in
front of the bench. He kept signaling to his bullpen for
Don Johnson and Joe Page to throw harder.

It looked like a rout for Boston when Johnson took
over. Billy Martin was one man on the Yankee bench
who still believed the game was not lost. He yelled at
his teammates when they were out on the field or
up at bat. He crouched on the dugout steps and
even heckled Ted Williams, Boston's Splendid Splin-
ter. With the Yanks eight runs behind in the seventh,
Casey Stengel, reaching for anything that would
change his team's luck, sent Billy out to second base in
place of Coleman. The Red Sox rooters jeered when
the public-address system announced the change. It
looked to them as if Casey had given up and was trying out his rookies.

A few minutes later Billy pulled Don Johnson out of
a hole by making a sparkling stop of a ball hit by Al
Zarilla, the Red Sox right fielder. It brought cheers
from the Boston fans, and when he ran in for the first
of the eighth, he yelled at his teammates, "Let's get the
big inning!"

He would be the fourth man up in the inning, and
knew full well that he would have to stand a going-over
from the Red Sox bench. Tebbets, working behind the
plate for Boston, was an expert at getting a hitter's goat.
He kept reminding himself, "Let them get the best of
you and you will soon be back in the minors." Yogi Berra
was the first man up and he hit Parnell for a single.

Billy got off the bench and went to the bat rack when Billy Johnson drew a base on balls. He would hit behind Lindell.

The crowd sat back, confident that Parnell would work himself out of the hole. The Red Sox could afford to give up a few runs this late in the game. Billy's lips were grimly set as he knelt in the on-deck circle. It was in his mind that this could be the best or the worst day in his life, his first time at bat in a big-league race.

Lindell flied out and the fans roared, but they howled with derision when Billy stepped up and faced Parnell.

Tebbets said, "He's sharp today, kid. You should've brought your glasses."

"I'll borrow yours, Pop," Billy shot back, his glance fixed on the tall Sox pitcher.

The Boston bench loudly asked if they starved ballplayers out in Oakland. Tebbets advised him to pull in his nose lest a fast ball knock it off. Remarks about his ears stung him, but he set his jaws tight and waited for the pitch he liked. It came in and he hit it to left field. Berra scored and Billy went on to second when the Red Sox outfielder threw to third base trying to cut Billy Johnson down. This would be one of the big thrills of Billy's life, his first official hit in the big leagues.

The rally continued. Henrich, Bauer, and Mapes kept it going. Billy was jitter-bugging in front of the Yankee bench, and yelling for the Bombers to keep hitting. He had them fired up. They more than batted around. Billy came to bat again in the inning and hit

Masterson, Parnell's relief for another single, driving in two more runs. Later he learned that he had set a record for a rookie playing in his first major league game. Fourteen men came to bat and nine runs came over the plate before the Yankees made their third out.

Boston rooters sat stunned. They hardly believed what they had seen.

Leading for the first time in the game, the Yanks took the field, grimly determined to hold it. Joe Page bore down on the Red Sox sluggers with Billy the Kid yelling at him every time he got set to pitch. He set Zarilla down but had to work much harder on Bobby Doerr, one of the better hitters in the league. Doerr drove one just inside second base with smoke on it, and Billy Martin cut to his right and scooped it up. His hurried throw got Doerr on a close play and Page, confident now, got Goodman to fly out.

The Yankees kept hitting and made Al Papai their fourth victim of the afternoon. They walked off Fenway Park with a 15-10 victory.

"With us that far behind," Casey said in the dressing room, "that fella wouldn't quit. He don't know the meaning of the word."

Crosetti grinned at Stengel. "Why, sure, Case. No Dago ever does."

Joe DiMaggio was the first to congratulate Billy. "Pretty good way to break in, kid," the slugger said. Some of the other veterans agreed with the Clipper, but the rookie knew he had not yet been accepted as a full-fledged Yankee. One game did not prove a man's ability. The writers for the Boston papers, however, gave him most of their attention while he dressed. Here was a colorful man, they had heard, a brash and temperamental kid, partial to noisy drama and free with his fists. They asked him if he thought he could stay with the Yankees and if he really got into those fights out on the coast.

"I think I'll stay," Billy said. "Maybe that sounds like bragging, but if you don't have confidence in yourself, who will? Sure, I got into fights but I didn't start them, and I won't run away from one."

Joe Page walked past and said, "Tell them how you tell us to play ball, kid."

He gave the writers a big grin as he pulled at the lapels of his new sports coat. "That wasn't exactly right." He became serious. "I've always been like that. Guys used to winning get careless, and being a man who hates to lose, I remind them to bear down. Sure, some of them get sore — but if it stirs them up, who cares? I've been a holler guy, I guess, ever since I picked up a ten-cent baseball."

Despite his showing in the first game, he appeared in only four games during the month of April. Up officially only three times, he had a batting average of .667. If his heart was heavy he gave no sign of it. He sparked the team from the bench; he was the busiest Yank in pre-game workouts. Bench warmer or not, he still wore the pin stripes of the Bombers and he still considered himself the luckiest man in the whole world.

Chapter VIII

As THE DAYS PASSED, Billy began to hear scraps of talk
in the Yankee dressing rooms about a player deal that
was about to take place. It seemed plain that he was to
be part of it, but he refused to believe it could be true
until George Weiss, general manager of the Yankees,
summoned him to his office.

"We're sending you to Kansas City, Martin," Weiss
said.

Billy stared at Weiss for several moments, the hot
Italian temper he had controlled since becoming a big
leaguer beginning to boil over. He left the office without a word and went looking for Casey Stengel. "I had
a good spring, Case!" he said when he found him.
"I've done everything I was expected to do. I never
thought you'd —— "

"Cool off, fella!" Stengel snapped. "Let me tell you
why we're sending you down. This is a business, Billy,
as well as a sport. We got this Stirnweiss and we can't
afford to lose him for no ten-thousand-dollar waiver
price, so Weiss figures to send you out for about three
weeks, sell Stirnweiss for twenty-five thousand dollars
and then bring you back."

"I shouldn't be going down and you know it, Case," Billy argued. "How many get brought back?"

"I don't own the club, Billy. If I were you, I'd keep still and go along with it."

Billy went to his hotel. He sat down and fought against the urge to go see Weiss again and tell him off. But he was hopping mad and was not thinking too straight. He went to Weiss' office again and it soon dawned on him that the general manager had never been too fond of him.

"I took a cut coming from Oakland to the Yanks," Billy told Weiss. "A three-thousand-dollar cut. It isn't fair your sending me to Kansas City. Somebody's going to be sorry."

"You talk fresh, Martin," Weiss snapped.

"I'm only fighting for my rights, Mr. Weiss," Billy retorted. "Make me a free agent. Other big-league clubs would be glad to get me."

"There is such a thing as a reserve clause, Martin," Weiss reminded the rookie. "And you have quite an opinion of yourself."

"I just know I'm a good ballplayer." He got up and left the office, his world seeming to fall out from under him. He packed his bags at the hotel and then looked up Joe DiMaggio. There were tears in his eyes and he was getting angry again when he said to the Clipper, "They'll pay for this someday."

"Look, Billy, you still belong to the Yankees, and I'm sure they want to hold on to you."

"A funny way of showing it," Billy choked out.

On his way out of New York, he was more determined than ever to show the Yankee organization they had made a mistake. He would play his heart out for the Blues.

The Kansas City players were suiting up for a game with Minneapolis when he walked into the dressing room. "Take your pick of the empty lockers, Martin," the clubhouse man said.

"It doesn't matter which one." Billy grinned. "I won't be here long."

His words proved to be true. He played just twenty-nine games for the Blues and hit .280. His spectacular fielding caught the fancy of the Kansas City fans and there was grumbling in the big city when the Yankees recalled him.

It was late July and the Bombers were trailing the Detroit Tigers by two games. When Billy the Kid put on the Yankee uniform again he heard that Billy Johnson was ready to be cut loose and that Brideweser was on the block. "What ails you guys?" he yelled at the other players. "You miss Old Billy that much?"

"Sure," Vic Raschi said, "like a pain in the neck." But he laughed and many of the other players joined in. Martin's presence here did something to all of them. His great fighting spirit and his confidence were something they needed.

They soon found out how valuable he was. Playing in his first complete game in Cleveland since his return from Kansas City, he made it plain to all present that he was soon to become the Yankees' regular second baseman.

In the second inning he made a diving stop of a hard grounder off Luke Easter's big bat and got up in time to throw the runner out. Going back to the Cleveland dugout, Easter looked back and shook his head. The game was close until the fifth, when Bob Lemon began to lose his skill. Zoldak came in to relieve him after Bobby Brown and Yogi Berra got on base.

Billy stepped in, and Jim Hegan, the Indians' catcher, said, "You remembered to buy a return ticket to K.C.?"

He turned and grinned at Hegan, then glared out at Sam Zoldak.

"Fire it past him, Sam!" a loyal fan shouted. "He can't hit!"

Billy took a strike, then a ball, and Zoldak reared back and threw one that looked big and fat. He swung hard and the thousands came to their feet when the ball sailed deep into the left field seats for a home run. His face was all smiles as he circled the bases. Berra and Brown reached for his hand as he crossed the plate. There was a standing welcome for him in the Yankee dugout. "You tagged that one, kid," Joe Di-Maggio said as he pumped the second baseman's hand.

The pennant race was the closest in the league for many years and every game counted. The Bombers went on to win it easily, and after the game a writer said to Stengel, "They look a whole lot better than they did their last trip, Case? Is it this Martin kid?"

Perhaps the answer came at the stadium a few days later in a pitching duel between Chuck Stobbs and Vic Raschi. Stobbs, a Bomber jinx, had given up but three hits when the Yankees batted in the last of the fifth. Billy Martin was the first man up and he looked at Crosetti and saw that the bunt sign was on. When Stobbs pitched, he shortened up and dumped the ball down the third-base line. It stayed fair and Pesky had no time to make a play. The fans started yelling for a rally.

Raschi also got the bunt sign and he hit it between the pitcher's mound and first base. Big Walt Dropo, the Boston first baseman charged in, then booted the ball. There were two men on when Gene Woodling came up. The outfielder drove a long fly to right center, and Billy cut loose after the catch and reached third. As Stobbs got set to pitch to Rizzuto, he knew the bunt sign was on again, and he took a daring lead off third.

The Scooter bunted and Billy set sail for the plate even as Stobbs turned the ball loose. He slid in safely with the run that made the difference and gave Raschi a 2-1 win.

The Yankees finally overhauled the Tigers and took a one-game lead on August 31st. They drove on to another pennant and beat the Phillies in four straight games in the World Series. Billy, who had played but thirty-four games that year and hit .250, took no part in the series sweep. While Jerry Coleman took over at second for Stengel, Martin was answering a call from his draft board out in Berkeley. Uncle Sam had need for Billy the Kid.

A few days before he put on his Army uniform, he married eighteen-year-old Lois Berndt in Berkeley, just an hour after he had played ball for Casey Stengel's All-Stars in the Oakland ball park. Always, it seemed, baseball came first in Billy's life. He served five months in the army until the Red Cross Chapter in his home town convinced the draft board that he was a hardship case. He was supporting his mother, his stepfather, his sister, and his wife.

Before he returned to the Yankees late in the 1951 season, he paid a visit to Father Dennis Moore. His marriage had not worked out as he had hoped. During the winter he had been involved in an automobile accident and had paid nearly three thousand dollars in damages. He was almost broke.

"I certainly need some advice, Father," Billy said to the priest.

"You work too hard at everything, Billy — except where your personal life is concerned. You have to get the best out of everything. Even a car's performance. You can't stand anything that's just average."

Billy grinned and admitted that Father Moore was right. "Sure, I have to have the best, or be the best, or I bust open inside."

The priest studied the ballplayer for a few moments. This man was easy to forgive, not to be blamed too much for his hurry to reach the top. He finally said, "I spoke to Lois, Billy. Most of her trouble is loneliness."

"I can't help being away so much. I'm a ballplayer."

"I understand. But make a big try at staying to- gether, Billy. And slow down a little or something will snap.

"I'll try. I promise," Billy said and caught himself drumming the arm of his chair with his fingers, a sign of impatience Father Moore knew only too well. Billy grinned a little sheepishly and got to his feet. "I'll send you a couple of tickets for the World Series next year, Father."

"One thing I'm sure you'll never lose, Billy," the priest said and smiled. "Your faith in yourself."

Billy felt lighter at heart when he left St. Ambrose's. What troubles he had left would disappear the mo- ment he got into a Yankee uniform again, when he heard the roar of the crowd, for baseball as far as he was concerned was his life.

Chapter IX

WHEN BILLY REPORTED to the Yankees late during the season of 1951, he seemed to have acquired even more confidence while in the army, along with a few pounds of weight. He found that all was not well with the Bombers. Figures showed that it was the second poorest hitting team in the history of the Yankees. Joe DiMaggio had had a poor season, and in July Stengel had removed the slugger from the line-up. Newspaper reports insisted that there had been hot words between Joe and the Yankee manager.

"Joe's mother died in June," Billy said as he donned the New York uniform once more. "He has a bad leg." He slammed a spiked shoe down. "It's always the way. Even the greatest are called bums when they start slipping a little."

Later he talked to Joe alone and realized that a big change had come over the Clipper. He had been playing on his nerve for weeks, he knew.

"Billy," Joe said, "when this game gets to be hard work instead of fun, it's time to retire. There's nothing sorrier-looking than a has-been trying to hang on."

"You'll be around another three years." Billy grinned. "You're a Dago."

"One more big series and it'll wind things up for me," DiMaggio said.

Stengel inserted his sparkplug into the Yankee line-up on August 2nd against Detroit. The Tigers, with hitters like Kell, Wertz, and Mullin, won the first game of the double-header, 9-8; but Casey Stengel was all smiles when the second contest got under way. The Bombers had started to hit again. He put Billy at shortstop and had him leading off at the plate.

A great stop of a ground ball hit by George Kell in the first inning showed Casey that Billy had lost none of his fielding skill while in the army. Tom Morgan, starting this game for the Yankees, grinned at the Yankee bench as he rubbed up the ball.

"All right, let's go-o-o-o!" the shortstop yelled.

Cain was pitching for the Tigers, and Billy hit him for a single his first time at bat. When he pulled up at first, the Yankees in the dugout began to make a lot of noise. They seemed eager to go up and hit, and drive Billy around. He scored later on a hit by Yogi Berra, his dark face split by a big grin when he took his seat in the dugout.

The Tigers began to hit Morgan, but Billy saved him in the fifth. With Kryhoski and Wertz on the bases for Detroit he stabbed a ball hit by Groth and fired it to Coleman. The second baseman threw to Collins for the double play.

Martin hit another single off Virgil Trucks who relieved Cain, and then slammed Gene Bearden who relieved Trucks, finishing up with a triple in the eighth. He had three hits for five times up, and scored three runs. He started two double plays that snuffed out Tiger rallies. He was the big gun for the Bombers in the 10-6 win.

Stengel, despite Billy's great showing in the double-header, used him sparingly for the remainder of the season. Billy sat on the bench on September 29th when the Bombers clinched the pennant by beating the Red Sox in two games at the stadium, the first one a no-hitter by Allie Reynolds. After the sixth inning Billy yelled at the Chief from the dugout steps with every pitch he made. Without picking up a bat or putting on a glove he was the busiest man on the field.

The Yankees finished up the season with another double-header against the Red Sox, and Billy played second base in the first contest and third base in the nightcap. He slammed out three hits and played error-less ball.

He had been in fifty-one games since coming out of the service and hit .259 and fielded .964. There were very few New York fans who would not admit his re-turn to the Yankees had been the real reason for their late-season drive for the American League flag.

Save for a pinch-hitting appearance, he sat out the World Series with the New York Giants, and suffered along with Joe DiMaggio who had gone to the plate eleven times without a hit. The Giants went ahead two games to one before the Clipper found the range. In the fourth game he hit a homer and a single; in the fifth contest, a double and two singles. The Yankees went on to win the series.

Billy was not ashamed of his tears when he watched

Casey Stengel put an arm around Joe in the dressing room and tell the Clipper he could not have won without him. It deepened his faith in Stengel, a man he was certain would never turn his back on a friend.

On December 11th, out on the coast, Billy read the news about the Clipper's retirement. Weiss, the writer pointed out, would have to make some kind of a deal to make up for the loss. The very sight or sound of the general manager's name gave Billy misgivings. He knew he was not one of Weiss' favorites, and the man's word was law. He could send any Yankee back to the minor leagues or another major-league club with one stroke of his pen.

When spring-training time came around, Billy knew he figured in the 1952 plans of the Yankees. He reported early, confident that this would be one of his best years — but strangely enough it was Joe DiMaggio who came close to putting an end to his career. Joe was engaged in a baseball promotional job for the American League, and led a camera crew to Miller Huggins Field in St. Petersburg, where he could take pictures of Yankee players for showings on TV screens.

Billy came running off the diamond when he spotted Joe talking to Stengel. "Hey, Joe, I knew you couldn't stay away from a ball park!" he shouted.

After they shook hands, Billy said, a grin at the corners of his mouth, "I'm moving into your locker when we get to the stadium, Joe."

"You're welcome," the Clipper laughed, then got down to real business. "Billy, I need a good action shot of a man sliding into base. How about it?"

"I'll be on television?" he asked, grinning from ear to ear.

"Sure. Even though you hate all that publicity, kid."

"Tell me when you're ready, Joe."

When the cameras were set, Billy took a short run, then hit the dirt. A few seconds later he was rolling over in the dust, his teeth grinding against the pain of a broken ankle. They carried him into the clubhouse, DiMaggio and trainer Gus Mauch following behind. The Clipper was close to tears and Billy forced a smile when he looked up him from the table. "Forget it, Joe. It wasn't your fault. It could have happened later in the season and that would have been worse."

A few days later, on crutches, Billy checked out of the Soreno. He was going to New York for a more complete examination and a long rest. For the next sixty days he became worried over rumors that he was going to be traded. During the first few games of the pennant race, he made less noise on the bench, and Casey Stengel watched over him like a mother hen, the wrinkles in his forehead deepening.

"Sure, Case," Billy said to Stengel in the clubhouse after Reynolds had won a close one from Cleveland, "keep smiling. It's good advice, but you wouldn't know what they're thinking right now in the front office, would you? Don't forget, they sent me to Kansas City when I was hitting good."

"Worry is something which never does a fella any good, Billy. It'll take weight off you which you can't afford. You sound like you want to quit."

Billy's eyes flashed their old fire. Stengel quickly walked away from him, a slow grin coming over his leathery face. He had long since discovered how to handle this kid from Berkeley. Or had he?

A day never looked sunnier than the one that found Billy Martin back in the Yankee line-up against the White Sox. In the third inning he drew a walk, and then set sail for third when Rizzuto, up with one out, hit a single to deep right. Halfway to the bag, he knew he would have to slide to beat the throw from the out-field. He went in head-first and felt the muscles in the back of his right leg give way. The pain made him a little sick as he rolled over, sweat glistening on his face.

When players came to help him he banged his fists against the ground. When would his bad luck end? Tears trickled down his face as he looked up at Frank Crosetti, the Yankee coach. "I guess that does it, Crow," he said as he let Gus Mauch get him to his feet. Now he was afraid. It could be the end of a lot of dreams. Only a few days ago word had come from Berkeley that he was going to be a father.

In the dressing room, while Mauch examined his leg, he blurted out, "I can go back and get a job in the steel mill, another slob carrying a dinner pail. I can sit up nights drinking beer and watching other guys play ball on television. My wife can go to work."

Mauch said, "Stop that kind of talk, Billy. This isn't bad at all." He turned toward the club physician.

"Gus is right, Martin," the doctor said. "A few more days you'll be playing again, as good as new."

Billy grinned. "I guess I acted like a school kid, Gus.

But I've got to stop running up doctors' bills for the Yankees."

"You can pay them back in the World Series," the trainer said.

He was getting into his street clothes when the Yankees filed in. "Remember to land on your head hereafter," Joe Collins said. "You couldn't get hurt that way."

Mickey Mantle laughed at him. "I'll get a wheelchair and take you to the movies, Billy."

Mantle had recently come up from Kansas City, a player due to fill the great DiMaggio's shoes. Billy and the outfielder had hit it off from the very first time they'd met.

He began laughing, his uneasiness gone. He knew he had been close to self-pity, something he hated in a man.

A few days after getting back into the line-up he could not get his mind off personal troubles. Anxiety gripped him. He had no appetite; his stomach always seemed to be tied in a knot. He found it hard to play through the last few innings of every ball game. At night his head would start spinning when he looked up into the lights. His legs seemed to carry weights when he ran for a ground ball. At night he could not sleep. Angry with himself, he tried to talk himself out of his despair. Was it insecurity? How could it be? He was a Yankee player, wasn't he?

One night in Connie Mack Stadium in Philadelphia, he dove to his right to knock down a hard drive off Elmer Valo's bat, but could not make the play to first. He felt like staying on the ground or going to the dugout to ask Old Case to relieve him. Hadn't Gus Mauch noticed the strain he was under?

He found out just two days later. The trainer approached him as he was reaching into his locker for his uniform. Mauch asked him how he felt.

"Fine, just fine," he replied and grinned.

"Get on the scales, Billy," Mauch ordered. "It's no use, mister. I talked to the waiter at the hotel. You've been signing meal tickets, but you don't eat. You've been living on hot lemonade and aspirin tablets."

Billy protested but Gus Mauch had his way. The trainer drew his breath in sharply and glanced at Stengel. "He weighs one-thirty-two, Case. He's lost thirty pounds. You trying to kill yourself, Martin?"

"I've just been off my feed," Billy said lamely. "Worrying a little, I guess." There was a trace of defiance in his dark eyes. Since he had come back to the line-up they had been shifting him from second to third, back to second, and then to shortstop. He would never complain, but to do his best a man had to stay at one position.

Gus Mauch was sure he knew the real trouble. Naturally high-strung, Billy did everything to the limit, even worrying. Gus had heard all about the ballplayer's youth, his fear of being anything but the best at his profession. He took Billy in hand and soon had him eating regularly, and prescribed mild sleeping pills.

Martin's explosive temperament was brought to the surface when the Yankees visited Boston early in June. Jim Piersall, a newcomer to the Red Sox, was playing shortstop in infield practice, and Billy and several of the Yankees were tossing the ball around in front of their dugout. Stories had gone the rounds that Piersall and Billy had started feuding in Florida during spring training.

Piersall kept yelling at Billy, calling him names, and the Yankee player tried his best to pay no notice until he heard one remark that his pride refused to let go by. His blood at the boiling point, he invited Piersall under the stands. The Red Sox outfielder, eager to oblige, followed Billy to the runway. Fists began to fly and Billy hit Piersall twice before Oscar Mellilo, the Red Sox coach, and Bill Dickey of the Yankees moved in to separate the two. Ellis Kinder, starting pitcher for the Red Sox that day, just managed to duck under a wild swing by Billy as he pulled the players apart.

Lou Boudreau, the Boston manager, no doubt blaming his player for starting the fight, benched Piersall for the afternoon. All during the game Piersall paced the Red Sox dugout, shouting at Billy. The man's actions seemed strange.

"What's got into the guy?" Billy asked Hank Bauer when he came back from a turn at bat. "Why would he hate me that much?"

Not long afterward Billy learned that Piersall had suffered a complete nervous breakdown and had gone to a hospital. Close to tears, he shouted at the writers, "How would I know Jim was that sick? I'll always be ashamed of that fight. You know I was on edge myself."

As the pennant race went down to the wire, news came from Berkeley that Billy had a daughter named

Kelly Ann. And a few days later he was notified that his wife, Lois, was seeking a divorce. His peace of mind shattered, Billy went into a crucial game against the Athletics on September 27th. Cleveland was pressing the Yankees hard and Casey Stengel needed one game to clinch the pennant.

Before he took the field, Billy looked at Old Case's anxious face and remembered how much he owed the man. Why, Case had really been a father to him. This was a ball game he wanted to help win for Old Case. He grinned as he watched Harry Byrd take the mound for the Athletics. What was it that Boston writer had said about Billy Martin? He always met the challenge of the moment.

For eight innings Byrd stopped the Bombers. Going into the ninth, the score was tied at 1-1. Mickey Mantle led off for the Yankees with a single. Billy jumped to his feet and yelled out at Byrd. "You've had it, Harry!" and the other Bombers joined in trying to unsettle the big right-hander.

Yogi Berra cracked a hit to the right side, but the Yankees' exciting yells broke off when Cass Michaels made a great stop of Mantle's bid for a single and forced Yogi at second. "Keep it alive, Joe," Billy yelled at Joe Collins. The first baseman answered him by getting his fourth hit of the afternoon, and sending Mantle around to third. Byrd, tiring, hit Hank Bauer on the arm and the bases were loaded.

Casey Stengel called McDougald back and sent Woodling in to hit for him, but the outfielder popped to short. It looked bad for the Yankees. Billy was afraid he would be called back when he walked to the plate, but Old Case went along with him. It was all the vote of confidence Billy needed.

Putting his troubles aside, he got set and waited for Byrd to pitch. He worked Byrd to a one ball and one strike count, then swung at a pitch and drove it into left field, driving in Mantle and Collins. The Yankees won the game, 3-1. They had also won the pennant.

Billy sat in front of his locker having a cool drink after being roundly congratulated by all the Yankees. The hit off Byrd had made up for a lot he had missed during the summer. It was an answer for George Weiss. It thanked Old Case for his belief in him.

The Yankees, hollering it up around him, knew he had won the ball game for them — but did they know he had been playing for weeks on his nerve alone? That his stomach had rebelled against everything he ate? That he was afraid his little daughter would grow up like he had, without really knowing a father? The big series with the Dodgers was less than a week away, competition that demanded full relaxation and a clear mind. At the moment he knew he had neither.

Yogi Berra leaned over and slapped him on the shoulder. "You must feel great, Billy. You did it for us."

"Sure," he said and gave Yogi his biggest smile. "I never felt better."

That night he ate very little. He had trouble getting to sleep.

Chapter X

WALTER ALSTON, manager of the Dodgers, and his veteran coaches made it plain that the only Yankees they had to stop to win the series was Mantle and Berra. They had overlooked the fact that big bats did not always win ball games, that a great glove man could be the difference. They did not worry over a second baseman who had only hit .267 in 109 games but who had batted nearly a thousand keeping up Yankee spirits and confidence. They had forgotten what another man with a fierce desire to win had once done for them. His name was Eddie Stanky.

The Dodgers battled the Yankees all the way in the big series. All even at three games apiece, the deciding game was played at Ebbets Field before an overflow crowd. They still talk about that game in Flatbush, where professional baseball is no longer played. It was won by the fiery little Yankee second baseman who hit only .217 in the seven games. Billy Martin. He won it in the field.

The Bombers were out in front 4-2 behind Vic Raschi when the Dodgers came to bat in the last of the seventh. The Dodger fans were screaming for a rally, and Carl Furillo, leading off, answered the cry by working a base on balls off the Springfield Rifle, Raschi.

Billy ran in and talked to Vic, and the Brooklyn fans booed and stamped their feet.

Rocky Nelson popped up, but Billy Cox, always dangerous in the clutch, clubbed Raschi for a single. Now the Dodger fans were on their feet and Casey Stengel was out in front of the dugout frantically signaling to the bullpen. Above the racket, Billy's voice could be heard as he shouted encouragement to Raschi. He ran in after Peewee Reese walked to fill the bases.

"All right, just throw it and we'll do the rest!" Billy shouted. "Bear down and let's get the winner's share."

Stengel, however, decided to remove Raschi. He came to the mound and signaled that he wanted Bob Kuzava to come in and pitch to the Dodger slugger, Duke Snider. One sweep of Snider's bat and it could be all over.

Kuzava, an effective relief pitcher all year, got the Duke to pop up to the infield. But an even more dangerous hitter was stepping up to the plate: Jackie Robinson.

Kuzava worked carefully on Jackie. With the count two balls and two strikes, he threw the batter a curve. Robinson seemed to hesitate before he swung. He hit the ball sky-high directly over the right side of the infield.

Billy let out a howl of glee, for it looked like an easy out. The ball belonged to Joe Collins at first, but suddenly Billy realized that Collins was not moving out of his tracks. He was looking up, but the sun, slanting across his face from the grandstand roof seemed to blind him. The Dodger fans were screaming themselves hoarse as the wind began blowing the ball in toward the plate. Brooklyn runners were on the move.

Billy stopped staring at Collins and broke away from second base. It seemed to every fan in the ball park that the ball would surely drop. He ran harder as the wind kept carrying the ball away from him. He ran out from under his cap, and at the last moment he made a desperate lunge, got the ball in his glove, and hung on. He was ten feet back of the plate before he could bring himself to a stop. The amazing play broke the Dodger threat and the Dodger spirit, and Kuzava stopped the Dodgers the rest of the way. Once more, the Yankees were champions of the world.

During the wild celebrating in the visitors' dressing room, Casey Stengel again reminded all present of Billy's value to the Yankees. "How about that kid's catch? If he don't do it, two runs cross the plate and the game is tied up. Maybe the Dodgers go on to win the game and the series."

"You forget he really won two of those games for us," Gil McDougald chimed in. "That one where he stole Dressen's squeeze-play sign with Pafko on third. The sign Dressen used in Oakland."

Billy looked up, grinned, and shook his head. "He changed it, Gil," he said. "I just watched Joe Black at the plate and knew the squeeze was on by the way Joe's eyes bugged out."

"So Reynolds pitched out," McDougald said after

the laughter had subsided, "and Yogi caught Pafko by more than fifteen feet. That run would have tied if it had come in. That warning yell of yours, Billy, was worth a lot of money to us. You keep on hollering."

The elation of victory wore off and Billy suddenly felt very tired and a little sick. His troubles came back to haunt him. In the light of what had happened, would he be a hero in the eyes of his mother and his sister Joanie? It seemed that the Martins were meant to have broken homes. He did not blame anyone, just kept wondering where he had failed. Father Dennis Moore had hinted that everything would have worked out fine if he hadn't been a ballplayer; but that was one thing he had to be, no matter what the cost.

He said good-byes to the Yankees as each player left the room. Stengel stopped him and asked what he intended to do during the winter.

"Some hunting, maybe, before I go back home, Case," Billy said.

"Get a lot of rest, fella," Stengel advised. "Get a little more weight on your bones. We'll need you next year."

The manager's words were sweet in his ears, but they would have been sweeter if they had come from George Weiss in the front office. There is a bogeyman always hanging around a ballplayer's locker. It represents the possibility of another player who can hit close to .300 coming up to take his place. A hitter has no security even though he can field well enough to stay out of another player's way. Crossing the bridge to New York, Billy realized that the pressure of big-league ball was harder than he had ever thought it would be, and he wondered if he would ever really adjust himself to the profession he had chosen for himself.

Was he expected to live up to the things they wrote about him? The Dead End Kid, The Agitator, a man anxious to swing his fists at the slightest excuse. He knew that he was none of these, but baseball fans are easy prey for the writers. He knew that if he were able to meet them all personally he could quickly change their minds about his being a real tough guy. Offhand he could not think of one person at the moment he actually disliked.

There was a good chance that he would be speaking to a group of youngsters sometime during the winter, and he knew what he'd be tempted to say:

"So you want to be a ballplayer? All right, you'll have to get used to playing in the summer when you sweat so much you can hardly hold a bat in your hands. You'll play when you're hurt and when you feel sick, because this game is a jungle where there's always somebody ready to take your job away from you. You'll take a lot of abuse from the fans and the enemy dugouts — and if you can't stand it, you will soon be back at the filling station or on the farm. There's a thousand other things I can think of that aren't glamorous if you'll give me a little time."

Billy grinned to himself and shook his head. If he had been told those things back on the sandlots he would have been a ballplayer just the same. He knew what he was going to tell young hopefuls. There wasn't a game in all the world like baseball. It was having fun and getting well paid for it, and it was a profession where every man had an equal chance, whether he was born in a city slum or in a mansion on a hilltop. But it was no game for a man who considered only the money involved, and didn't care whether he won or lost. Of course it was a business, but it was also the national game of the United States of America.

Billy Martin will always remember the 1953 pennant race as something of a nightmare. For the better part of the season he was tormented by old injuries and letters from his wife's lawyers pressing for a divorce. Unthinking fans heaped abuses on his head and even accused him of deserting his wife and baby. When he came off the field in Chicago's Comiskey Park one afternoon, a baby bottle was thrown at his feet. "Go home and feed your family, you no-good!" a fan shouted at him. That morning a local paper had printed a story saying that Billy's family was suffering hardships at home. Nothing had ever been further from the truth.

In the dressing room after the game, he had to fight back the tears that burned his eyes. He walked the floor, asking himself why people would deliberately print lies about him. Flying spikes had never hurt him more. He said to Stengel, "You don't believe that, do you? Look, Case, every month I send her —— "

"You don't have to ask me that, Billy," Stengel said, putting a hand on the player's shoulder. "Forget it, kid. There have to be vultures in the world. Some people would sell their souls to put something in print."

He nearly fell into a state of deep depression as the pennant race went into August, but it was not apparent to his teammates. He played on sheer courage alone and assured his best friends, Mantle and Whitey Ford, that he would murder them if they breathed a word to Casey Stengel about his sleepless nights and visits to the drugstore.

If Gus Mauch, the Yankee trainer, had any suspicions he kept them to himself, for Billy was hitting around his normal average and coming up with the plays in the field when they were needed. He was batting in more runs than he ever had since coming to the Yankees.

In Philadelphia on August 16th, he felt like telling Casey Stengel to rest him, for he was sure he could not last nine innings. His hands shook when he gripped a bat. They were cold and moist. His legs felt weak under him. In the third inning he threw a ball off Harry Byrd's bat over Joe Collins' head for an error. When he left the dugout in the top of the eighth to wait in the hitter's circle, Stengel called him back.

"You feel all right, Billy?"

"Why not, Case? I'll show you I'm all right."

Gene Woodling had doubled and was on second. Noren singled and Woodling came around to score. The Yankees were in front by one run. Up with runners on, Billy slammed Byrd's pitch into the upper left deck and came around with the run that gave his team a three-run margin. Four runs scored in the inning and when the Athletics came in, they were trailing 8-4. They started hitting Gorman, and Stengel called in Allie Reynolds. The Chief was also driven out of the box and the Athletics tied the game up, 8-8. They won it in the ninth and Billy stormed around the visitors' dressing room kicking loose everything that was not nailed down.

"What a game to lose!" he yelled. "What were the pitchers throwing, Case? Melons?"

"We got to lose one now and then," Stengel said.

"Why do we?" Billy retorted and fired a sweat sock across the room.

Whitey Ford said to Mickey Mantle as he brushed past the slugger, "I'd say he was perfectly healthy, Mick."

It was far from the truth. When the Yankees came back for a stand against the Western clubs, Billy paid daily visits to St. Patrick's Cathedral which, he told his friends later, saved him from a complete breakdown.

One morning, after Mass when he came down the steps of the church, a man stopped him. "Are you Billy Martin?" he asked. The player nodded and smiled pleasantly.

"All right," the man shouted at him. "If you're a member of this parish, I'm going to quit!"

Billy walked away, swallowing his resentment. And then he remembered this was the year when Yankee haters were really making themselves heard. It could have happened to any of the other players. How could people judge others without really knowing them? He thought of the grandmother who had understood him better than anyone else in the world. He could almost hear her voice saying, "Bellino, you look at me. Did you go to work at the church today?" It seemed so long ago that she had lived.

He kept up his late-season "clutch" hitting when men were on the bases. Against Cleveland with only two weeks left in the race, Early Wynn stopped him for seven innings. With the Yanks two runs behind, he waited in the on-deck circle and watched Joe Collins draw a walk. Bauer flied out to Doby, but Woodling singled, sending Collins to second. This was the time, he thought, to get that hit. He had read something once he'd never forgotten: Think so and it will be.

He hit Wynn's second pitch to left and scored Collins, and when the throw from the outfield got away from Avila, Woodling went to third, and Billy streaked for second. The Yankees won the game 4-3, pinch-hitter Johnny Mize driving in the winning run.

The Bombers drew away from the rest of the teams in the stretch drive and won the pennant. Bill finished with an average of .257 for 149 games; 75 per cent of his hits were singles, but he drove in seventy-five runs, more than any of the Yankees except Berra, Mantle, and McDougald. His fielding average was .983, playing three positions: second, third, and short.

It was a year Billy would always remember, and in some ways he would like to forget.

Chapter XI

Deep anxiety gripped him the night before the opening game of the World Series at Yankee Stadium. He walked the canyons of New York, for he dared not sit still in any one place too long lest he think too deeply of his troubles. When he met some of the other players he put on that smile few people could ever resist, and a few minutes in his company took all the tension out of a man. He was also the spirit of the Yankees off the diamond.

It was late when he finally got to sleep, his last thought a frightening one: What if he collapsed on the field in front of seventy thousand people?

Inwardly as nervous as a cat, his olive-skinned face a little drawn, Billy gave the Dodgers not the slightest sign that he was worried about anything during pregame workouts. He was as noisy as ever and Stengel seemed to enjoy hearing him taunt players like Gil Hodges, Snider, and Campanella. Once Campy walked past the Yankee dugout and grinned in at Billy. "Don't you come at me like an express today," he said laughingly, "or I'll turn you into a local."

"Oh, but you're getting fat, Campy," Billy shot back, a big smile on his face. He glanced at Jackie Robinson who was examining a glove in front of the Brooklyn bench, and felt great admiration for the Negro star for more reasons than one. After he had baited Jackie just before that exhibition game with Brooklyn in 1950, Yankee haters had spread the lie that he was prejudiced, and Jackie had been the first person to defend him. "Billy is none of the things they call him. He's always looking for a way to win, the kind of player that's a pain in the neck, and smart and daring. He'll find the way to beat you."

It suddenly occurred to Billy that no word in his behalf had come from the Yankee front office at the time, not even from the majority of the players. But this was no time to dwell on such things. He kept moving around. The palms of his hands were clammy and he kept wiping them on the front of his uniform.

Crosetti, the veteran coach, shouted as the Yankees took the field, "Let's get them. It's only another ball game."

Just another game! Trotting out to his position, Billy knew a lot of money was at stake here. One player could fold up and knock over the rich apple cart, a player going along on his nerve and wondering if old injuries would shackle him. He caught himself wishing that Casey had started someone else instead, then felt angry at himself. He'd never quit until they carried him off.

His piping voice was plainly heard above the crowd's

roar when Junior Gilliam came up to lead off for the Dodgers. His legs felt shaky under him, and he hoped the Yankees would quickly get off to a long lead. Less than three hours later he was sitting in the clubhouse, one of the heroes of the first game finally won by Johnny Sain's relief pitching, 9-5. He had made three hits and had fielded without an error. It seemed unreal, for he hardly remembered the things he had done.

He joined in the merriment. "How come their fielders played me so shallow?" he yelled. "Didn't their scouts tell them I was ten pounds heavier this year?"

Outside the stadium, hundreds of fans lingered to get a close look at their idols and most of them shouted praise for Billy. One loud voice came out of the crowd, "You lucky stiff, Martin, you won't get a scratch hit in the rest of the series."

At the hotel he felt very weary. The hostile fan's prophecy could easily come true, for he had played that first game in a kind of walking trance. Deeply religious, he was certain of one thing: God had held his bat that afternoon.

His two hits, one a home run, helped the Yankees make it two in a row the next afternoon. It looked like a clean sweep for the Bombers, for they had beaten Preacher Roe, 4-2. And then the scene shifted across the river to Ebbets Field, where Carl Erskine kept the Dodgers alive with a 3-2 victory over Vic Raschi. One of the six hits he gave up was to Billy Martin. Stengel called upon Whitey Ford to win the fourth game, but he was anything but sharp and took a 7-3 loss. But Billy Loes could not stop the amazing Yankee second baseman who got two hits off him, one a booming triple. Billy was leading the Yankee hitters with eight safeties in the first four games.

The fifth game was a slugfest, with Jim McDonald, Stengel's fifth pitcher finally being given the win, 11-7. Billy hit a single and a home run and led both clubs with ten hits.

"It don't go more than six games," Old Case said in the dressing room. "The way that feller is hitting. And what is he doin' with the glove? Only a thousand. Tomorrow Whitey Ford will finish it and we can all go home."

Swarmed over by writers and jubilant Yankee players, Billy was more more amazed than anyone over his success. Now he was dead certain he was getting outside help. All of his prayers were being answered. Physically he had been struggling through, and his mind had hardly been at ease. He figured he would pay a price when it was over. Next year, he mused with a grim smile, so would Mr. Weiss.

The laughs he got out of the newspaper accounts of the series lifted his spirits and bolstered him up for the next ball game. Walter Alston, the manager of the Bums, said he had heard somewhere that Billy Martin had been in poor shape at the end of the season, and wondered what he would have done to his club if he had been in perfect health. His team, he moaned, was getting murdered by a .257 hitter. But there was a law of averages and his pitchers would stop him the rest of the way.

It was wishful thinking on Alston's part. In the sixth game at Yankee Stadium, Billy stepped up for his second turn at bat and drove out his eleventh hit of the series. His next time up he smashed the ball off Junior Gilliam's leg and the scorers gave the Yankee second baseman an error. Afterward Bill Dickey and the whole Yankee bench raved over the decision. "You should sue them for grand larceny, Billy," Dickey said angrily.

"Maybe they figure I've got too many hits now, Bill," the second baseman grinned. "It could go to my head."

The Bombers led, 3-1, going into the ninth, but Carl Furillo smashed a home run off Allie Reynolds, who had relieved Ford in the eighth, driving in Duke Snider ahead of him. The weather had turned raw and cold when the Yankees came in for their turns at bat. The lights were turned on. The Dodger fans were screaming for Labine, who had come in to take over for Carl Erskine to hold down the Yankees and go on to win.

Labine walked Hank Bauer, and Yankee fans implored their favorites to put on a typical Yankee finish. Yogi Berra came up and lined out to Furillo, but Mickey Mantle beat out a slow roller to third. When Billy Martin stepped into the batter's box, a thunderous ovation came pouring out of the stands. He had sparked the Yankees at bat and in the field throughout the series. They yelled for him to get a hit although they were well aware that the odds were against him.

Billy was not concerned with the odds. He had a feeling that he would come through. Think so and it will be.

The first pitch was a ball. He dug his spikes into the dirt, his feet planted wide, cocking his bat menacingly at Clem Labine. The Dodger bench jockeys did their level best to rattle him. Labine reared back and threw him a fast ball, a little low. Billy swung and drilled the ball past the pitching mound, over second base and into the outfield for his twelfth hit! Hank Bauer raced in with the winning run, whooping it up as he rounded third.

The Yankee players poured out of the dugout to get Billy. He had given them the winning share of the biggest World Series gate in history. For the second straight year they had to thank him for it. They mauled him, hugged him, and literally carried him into the clubhouse.

Inside, it was bedlam. "How did it feel, Billy?" someone shouted.

"The greatest thrill I ever had," he said, hardly believing what had happened. "I don't exactly know what I was thinking up there, except that I had to get that run home." He was tempted to say more, to remind them all — even Mr. Weiss, who was shouldering his way through the excited celebrants to shake his hand — that he was throw-in material the time the Yankees made the deal with Oakland to get Jackie Jensen. But he guessed they would be remembering.

George Weiss congratulated him. He told Billy he

was great, and the ballplayer grinned, hoping the front-office brass would not forget too soon. John Drebinger, the New York *Times* sports writer, said to him, "You know you broke one of Babe Ruth's records, Billy?"

Billy stared at the man, his mouth opening wide. "You're crazy," he said.

"All right," Drebinger said. "Read the papers tomorrow."

Going down to breakfast the next morning, Billy discovered he had become a real celebrity, a popular idol. He read all the New York papers that day and discovered that he had played havoc with old records and set new ones. The October, 1953, World Series book on him read:

Holds World Series record for most hits, six-game series (12), 1953; broke Babe Ruth's (New York Yankees 1923) mark for most total bases, six-game series (23), 1953; tied the following series records in 1953, Davy Robertson's (New York Giants, 1917) mark for highest batting average in six-game series (.500) by getting twelve hits in a series, a mark held by four other players; tied George Rohe's (Chicago White Sox, 1906) and Bob Meusel's (New York Yankees, 1923) record of two triples in a six-game series, and tied with Babe Ruth (New York Yankees, 1923), Chick Hafey (St. Louis Cardinals, 1930) and Junior Gil-

*liam (Brooklyn Dodgers, 1953) for most long hits
in a six-game series.*

He sat on top of the baseball world. He was toasted
at "The Store," Toots Shor's restaurant, at Harwyn's,
and all the places where important people gather. But
reaction soon took hold of him, for basking in the spot-
light could never overcome physical strain or cause
domestic troubles to disappear.

He received nearly twenty thousand dollars' worth
of TV and testimonial offers, but had to turn good fortune down. All he wanted at the moment was to go
home for a complete rest. He knew the only place he
could find it was in the house on Berkeley's Seventh
Street. Hero worship would wear off during the winter, and in the spring he would be just another ballplayer fighting promising rookies for his job.

The neighborhood where he had been born had
undergone little if any change. The years seemed to
fall away from him as he approached the two-story
house, and he was a little somber-faced Italian boy
again, afraid of what Nona would say and do when
she saw he had ripped his pants again.

Joy moved into the Martin household with Billy's
return. He picked up his mother and held her tight and
said laughingly, "Ma, you've been eating too much
pizza." His sister Joanie clung to him. She had grown,
he was sure, a head taller. "You get prettier every

day," he told her and gave her a present he had brought from New York.

"I'm so proud of you, Billy," Joanie said, happy tears making her dark eyes shine. "At school they talk about you all the time. The boys say you are the best ballplayer on the Yankees, in all the world."

Jack Downey smiled at him. "Like old times, Billy," he said. "Maybe we can go duck hunting. We'll —— " He had to stop and catch his breath, for his illness had been getting steadily worse. Excitement was not good for it.

"No," Billy said. "I'm a tired man, Jack. I haven't been feeling too good myself."

"I noticed when you came in," his mother said, a worried look in her eyes. "A kind of fever you got? You hardly touched your food. Maybe you go right to bed."

"And I'll stay there," Billy said.

He did not come downstairs until a week later. One day his mother brought his little daughter, Kelly Ann, to see him. She seemed a little afraid of him at first, and it was like sharp spikes going through his heart. "How Nona would have loved this little kid," he said and looked at his mother, a question in his eyes.

"I talk to her, Billy, but it is no use. She say, can she stay in love with a newspaper clipping?"

"I can't blame her," Billy said. "I guess some ballplayers should wait a long time before they get married."

Booster clubs around San Francisco Bay presented the Yankee second baseman with two automobiles for his big 1953 World Series. One of them, worth five thousand dollars, he gave to Father Dennis Moore.

"You can get around more in that, Father," Billy said. "Look how many more souls you can save. It will make up for the times I did not show up here to sweep up. And I know that what I did in the series was not just on my own. I had help."

"We're all proud of you, Billy," the priest said. "You have no idea what your success has meant to the boys in this neighborhood. They know they have as big a chance as anyone else to make dreams come true."

"Thanks, but I haven't played it too smart, Father."

"I'm glad to hear you say that, Billy Martin. Humility in a man is a very good thing."

Billy laughed. "I'm glad a lot of ball players don't see it in me. They'd really drive me out of the ball parks."

Honors kept coming his way. A few weeks later he was notified that he had won the Babe Ruth Memorial Trophy as the outstanding player in the 1953 World Series. But early in 1954 the pendulum swung the other way.

Chapter XII

BILLY MARTIN received a notice to report to his draft
board at Berkeley, and at first he wondered if someone
was playing a joke on him. When he presented himself before the board, he was given the blunt facts.

"But I still have five dependents," he protested. "If
my hardship case applied in 'fifty-one, it does now.
Why shouldn't it?"

"You have been very successful since that time, Martin," the head of the board said. "You're a big star and
you have made a lot of money. We believe you're in a
position to serve your country."

"Why didn't you leave me in the army the first
time?" Billy yelled at the man. "I'm a ballplayer and
only have a few years to build up any kind of security.
Two years out of my life means — I'll fight this all the
way. If a war was on, I wouldn't complain, but this
looks like it's being done out of spite."

"That's not so, Martin, and you know it," the head
of the board told him.

Billy fought against induction in vain. The draft

116

board, a lot of the fashionable people in Berkeley, and Yankee haters all over the country wrongfully judged him. A lot of idol worshipers had turned into a wolf pack overnight, calling him a slacker. A San Francisco newspaper received over 300 letters containing unfair criticism of the Yankee ballplayer.

He was sent to Camp Ord, California, and soon complained of the treatment given him there. He sent a letter to Congressman William Hess of Ohio, chairman of a committee investigating "special treatment" of athletes in the armed forces. He charged that officers at Ord were hounding him for no good reason, giving him extra duty and the most menial details. The letter was released for publication and fans all over the country, believing what they wanted to believe, labeled him a sorehead and a brat spoiled by a Yankee reputation. The adverse publicity alarmed the New York Yankee front office.

Hess made an investigation, the result being that Billy was transferred to Camp Carson in Colorado.

Billy would never stop fighting when he honestly believed he was right. At Carson he continued to voice resentment against his draft board, and insisted he could prove his family would suffer if he lost two years in the big leagues.

George Weiss suggested that Mickey Mantle, in the interest of Yankee public relations, go to Camp Carson and try to calm Billy down. It proved a wise move.

Mantle, after a long talk with his old roommate,

went to the army base's Public Information Office and spoke with Captain William Newkirk.

"What do I think of Martin?" the officer said. "I can't understand what I read about him, Mickey. He's an entertaining and generous fellow, and everybody here likes him. I believe he'll settle down now and make the best of things. He's taken charge of the baseball team here and wants to coach a couple of Little League clubs in the area."

A few months later Mantle got a letter from Billy. He passed it around the Yankee clubhouse just before they took the field against the Red Sox.

"I like the army now, Mick," Billy wrote. "I'm a killer and shoot a tommy-gun. I mop floors like anybody else. What do you think, they made me a corporal and gave me a good-conduct medal. I'll bet nobody in the American League will believe that. And what's the matter with that ball club? You need Old Billy that bad? Fifth place! Old Case must be out of his mind."

The Yankees did not win the pennant that year, 1954. Baseball writers blamed it on the absence of Billy Martin. Without the spark, an engine's battery runs down. The pitchers missed his high-pitched, encouraging voice when things got rough. The hitters needed his urging from the bench. Even Casey Stengel, they said, seemed to lack his old fire without the peppery second baseman there to make the Yankees go.

Billy read these things in the barracks and he had to

chuckle. Yesterday they wanted his scalp. Today he was something of a hero once more.

Late in 1955 a story in the New York *Daily News* was headlined:

ARMY TO THE RESCUE. Martin to Join Yanks!

It was a great if laugh-getting tribute to Billy. It was bad news for the rest of the American League. The Yankees looked as if they were to lose their second pennant in a row. They were staggering along, fighting to hold on to a slim lead. Billy's arrival in Kansas City a few days later prompted a celebration in the Bombers' dressing room.

"You know what?" Billy shouted as he undressed. "They gave me an honor guard when I left the camp."

"They wanted to make sure you got out and stayed out," Whitey Ford said.

"I'd better stay out or you guys will blow the pennant again," Billy shouted back. "It was good for me in the army. I gained a lot of weight. Listen, my ball team won seventeen of nineteen games. I hit .585 and played second, short, and in the outfield. I even pitched and did good. Case, if you need a pitcher for the late innings —— "

His presence had the effect of a bright light suddenly appearing in the darkness. Strain began to fall away from the sunburned faces of the Yankee players.

Laughter was the best medicine and Billy could provoke it. He had them all laughing with tales of army life. His spirit was what they needed. He was the guy who would get them going again.

They went out and crushed the Kansas City Athletics, 11-6. Billy prodded them from the bench, for Stengel wanted him to take a day or two to get the feel of a big-league diamond again before he took over his old position. Before the game with the Senators on September 2nd, Stengel called a secret meeting of the Yankee players. He laid down the law and demanded better results from all of them or changes would take place before next year. Then he turned Billy Martin loose on them.

"Look," Billy said, "you've been playing like bushers, like you wanted to lose. I had three cars when I went into the army. Now I haven't got one. I'm broke and I've got a family to support. We've got to get in that World Series. Oh, I know I won't get much out of it, but it'll be more than I got in the army." He paused and gave them a withering look they knew so well.

"I'm glad I wasn't there last year because you all know how I hate to lose. I told those guys at Carson the Yankees would win the pennant this year, so don't make a liar out of old Billy."

He got a great ovation when he took over at shortstop for the Yankees. Casey had him batting third, and in the first inning he flied deep to Roy Sievers in left field. He had hit the ball hard and knew somehow that he would get a lot of hits before the race was over. He faced Bob Porterfield in the third and hit a double, but Berra could not bring him in.

The Senators could not get a scratch hit off Ford for the first few innings. Porterfield was going strong for the Senators until Billy led off in the sixth. He clubbed a single, his second hit, and raced to third when Berra also hit safely to right. He yelled down at Mickey Mantle who was at the plate, "Hit it good. Hit it all the way."

Mantle celebrated his roommate's return by driving the ball out of the park.

Whitey Ford gave up but one hit to the Senators and won it, 4-0.

Billy had not had one chance in the field and Stengel yelled at O'Day, writer for the New York *Daily News*, "They didn't dare hit it toward that fella."

Once again it was happening. With Billy Martin, the Yanks drew away to a three-and-a-half-game lead over Cleveland on September 22nd. Billy was hitting close to .300. That day in the fifth inning with Collins and Elston Howard on base, he hit a home run off Abernathy, the Senators' pitcher.

The Yankees won nine of their last ten games in 1955, clinching the pennant on September 24th. They beat the Red Sox, 3-2, behind Larsen. Billy Martin got two hits off Nixon to lift his average for twenty games to an even .300. His fielding average, due to a long layoff, was .970, a little under par. But his very presence more than made up for his few miscues in the field.

"Sure, superstition is a part of baseball players," a

writer said to Casey during the pennant-clinching party. "Is Martin such a difference or is it just coincidence?"

"That fella can shame others into winning," Casey
said. "He never went to college but he's smart. He
doesn't have to think two seconds to do the right thing
at the right time. He can play three positions and hits
when it counts. Let's say he is a valuable fella, one who
makes a manager's job easy."

"I'll say it like I generally do, Case. Billy Martin is
the kid that sparks the Yankees. Haven't they always
looked bad without him?"

Whitey Ford faced Don Newcombe in the first game
of the World Series at Yankee Stadium. In the sixth
inning, after Collins had hit his second home run of
the afternoon, Bill hit Newcombe for a triple. A few
moments later he tried to steal home and was blocked
off by Campanella. The big catcher tagged Billy on the
neck and then fell on top of him. When he got up he
threw his arms around Campy, his temper getting the
best of him. Suddenly he told himself that the World
Series was no place for a brawl, and he let go of Campy and walked to the dugout.

The Dodger fans booed him and he took it without
resentment. "I just lost my temper for a moment," he
said when he settled down on the bench, happy at the
thought he was learning to control it.

The Dodgers gave the Yankees a scare in the eighth.
Trailing by three runs, Furillo led off with a single to
center. After Hodges had flied to left, Jackie Robinson

stepped up to face Ford. He let a pitch go by for a ball, then took a strike. He slashed at the third offering and hit a grounder that McDougald failed to stop. While the ball rolled into left field, Furillo raced to third and Jackie to second.

Billy came in and talked to Whitey. "This guy Zimmer is easy. You're as good as out of it," he said.

Zimmer hit a long fly to center and Furillo tagged up, then scored easily. Jackie, after the catch, took off for third and beat the throw-in. Alston sent Frank Kellert in to pinch-hit for Bessent who had relieved Newcombe. Everybody in the ball park had their eye on Jackie Robinson. The great Dodger infielder had stolen home many times. Billy kept yelling, "Watch him!" as Jackie took big leads off third.

Ford wound up, and Jackie tore for home. Yogi caught Ford's hurried throw but Robinson slid under him and scored the fifth run. Bob Grim finished up for Casey Stengel and held on to a 6-5 victory. Billy Martin, continuing his amazing World Series hitting, had two hits for three times at bat.

Tommy Byrne beat the Dodgers, 4-2, the following afternoon, allowing only six hits; but the Dodgers, fighting mad, took a two-run lead off Bob Turley in the third game of the series. It could be a jinx, for they had taken a two-run lead in every ball game. But Podres, the stylish left-hander for Alston, held the Yankees at bay while the Brooklyn attack racked up eight runs. Staying hot, the Dodgers won the next two 8-5 and 5-3, and the Yankees found themselves with their backs against the wall. But they would be back in their home park, with Ford ready to go.

Whitey beat the Brooks, 5-1, and it would be up to Tommy Byrne to keep the championship of the baseball world in New York. For three innings neither side could get a run across the plate, but in the fourth hits by Hodges and Campanella gave Brooklyn a 1-0 lead. They added another run in the fifth and time was running out for the Yankees.

"Let's get going!" Billy yelled when he led off in the sixth. He worked Podres for a walk, and McDougald bunted for a base hit. The Yankee fans had something to cheer about for the first time in the ball game. There were two on, nobody out, and the ever-dangerous Yogi Berra up at the plate. Billy, taking his lead off second, shouted in at Yogi, "Bring us in, Yog! Circle all the bases!"

Berra hit one of Podre's pitches to deep left and a great roar welled out of the packed stadium and fanned out over the Bronx. Billy tore around third, but halfway to the plate, he heard Crosetti yelling at him. He put on the brakes and looked out toward the left-field corner just in time to see Sandy Amoros make the greatest catch of the series. Billy raced back to third, but McDougald never got back to first base. Peewee Reese took the throw from the outfield and fired to Hodges, doubling up Gil to break the back of the Yankee rally.

Billy squirmed and fumed on the bench as he watched Podres make short work of the Yankees in the

ninth, setting down Skowron, Cerv, and Elston Howard, one-two-three. He quickly headed for the runway
when the Dodgers swarmed over the infield to carry
Podres off the field.

Although he had slammed out eight hits in the series
for a .320 average and fielded a thousand, Billy could
not be consoled in the dressing room. He blamed the
loss on himself. He should have had more than one hit
off Podres, especially in the seventh when the left-
hander blew a fast ball by him. He went to a far corner
of the room and cried. He hit the lockers with his fists.

"One hit could have turned that game around," he
said angrily. "I should have my head examined. I forgot to think. Podres was throwing change-ups all afternoon. I should have known he'd throw fast balls when
it got darker. I never want to feel the way I do now
ever again."

"Take it easy, Billy," someone called out. "You can't
personally win for the Yankees all the time."

His head snapped up. His lively dark eyes shot
sparks. "Why not? That's what I want to do. If I can't
have the best, I don't want anything."

Stengel said, "It was that little fella, Amoros. Alston
made a smart move sending Gilliam in from left to
play second and putting that Amoros out there."

"You know," Berra said, "if Sandy had not been left-
handed, he never would have made that catch. If he'd
had to back-hand it, he could never have held on to
the ball."

"Just the same," McDougald said, "I never thought he'd do it. I sure felt like a chump when Reese doubled me up."

The Yankee players met a few days later to vote on the players' shares of the series, and did an unprecedented thing. They paid tribute to the scrappy little infielder who had lifted them out of depression and put them back on top of the American League once more, by voting Billy Martin a full share of the series money, even though he had appeared in only twenty games during the regular season.

He needed the money badly. It was like a gift from heaven. Billy thanked them all with tears in his eyes, and that night, he told Mickey Mantle, "An awful lot of people hate the Yankees, Mick. They just don't know them. How can you hate guys who did a thing like this for me?"

Chapter XIII

BILLY'S READY WIT, his famous smile, and his magnetic personality made him one of the most popular after-dinner speakers in the business of baseball. Following a tour of Hawaii and Japan with a group of All-Stars after the 1955 World Series, he appeared at over 120 "booster" banquets throughout northern California. It was great publicity for the Yankees. Even out of uniform he was one of their greatest assets.

In front of an audience one night consisting mostly of boys who had played on their area high school teams, he made it clear that playing second base was not simply standing out there and waiting for a ball to come your way.

"There's a million things to remember," Billy said. "I never go out to the bag without looking at the grass to see if it's wet. Wet grass slows the ball up and you have to jump it faster. I look at the flags to see which way the wind is blowing — every inning. I hate dark glasses, so I look up at fly balls out of the corners of my eyes. But you have to know where the sun is all the time. You have to know the batters and learn to watch their feet. You shift accordingly . . . "

Always they asked him about Mickey Mantle. Did he and Mick snap their fingers at the Yankee curfew? Were they Broadway playboys?

Always he had to laugh. "There's nothing to those stories," he told them. "Our night life is mostly paying visits to our favorite spots and having a beer or two. We both love the movies, and when we go we always keep an empty seat between us if we can. Mantle eats chocolate bars and I don't like it on my clothes. I wave my arms around when I get excited."

A man of quickly changing moods, he began to fret when his speaking tour was over, when he had time to think. It was about time for the Yankee front office to mail out players' contracts. When his arrived he looked it over quickly, then sent it back. It called for sixteen thousand dollars.

"Is that smart, Billy?" his mother asked. "Such a lot of money!"

"I deserve more, and they know it," he said. "Look, Mama, I've started a fund for Kelly Ann's education. Joanie will be ready for college before you know it, and I want her to pick any one she wants. Maybe an expensive Eastern school. When I see her graduate I'll know baseball paid off. And I want to fix up this house and see that Jack gets the medical care he needs."

"And if they do not pay you more?"

"You stop worrying." He put an arm around her and drew her close. "You just wait and see if old Billy isn't right."

The Yankee front office was cool to his demand for a raise, and while the Bombers began working out in St. Petersburg, Billy went to New York and settled down in the Hotel Edison to wait. He soon discovered that Yankee fans were solidly behind him. At Shor's and all other places frequented by big-league players they encouraged him to hold out. Writers could not understand why Weiss was bickering with the player who had contributed so much to the success of the Yankees.

The Yankees finally offered him twenty thousand dollars and he signed. When he arrived in St. Petersburg a small army of baseball writers cornered him at the Soreno. They found him cautious, and they became aware of the signs of growing maturity on his face. An attempt to draw him out, to get him to pop off against George Weiss and other Yankee executives, was wasted.

"I'll only say I'll go along doing the best I know how," he said, disarming them with a sunny grin. "I'll remember the mistakes I made. They still say I'm the sparkplug of the Yankees. Remember, I never said it."

When he put on the pin-stripe uniform for his first workout, Mickey Mantle said, "I was talking to Daniel, Drebinger, and those other guys, Billy. They said you've changed." Mantle put the last half of a chocolate bar in his mouth and laughed. "Oh, sure. Once when I was a kid I picked up a firecracker I thought had fizzled out. It blew up in my hand."

As spring training progressed, Billy's conduct on and off the field was everything to be desired; but when it came time to break camp and move north, old worries began to creep into his mind again. Old injuries might flare up and slow him down. Stengel had a pair of infielders who had looked like great prospects in the exhibition games. The thing that bothered him most was the persistent rumor going the rounds that Casey Stengel and George Weiss were very much at odds. He felt certain he was the reason for it. He took this mental hazard into the 1956 pennant race.

He played steady ball for the first few weeks, bearing in mind every minute that even the slightest breach of conduct could be his downfall. But there are times when even the mildest-mannered ballplayer loses his self-control. On May 22nd in Kansas City, he became the key figure in a rhubarb that nearly led to a riot on the field.

The Athletics started their rookie pitcher, Santiago, to oppose Don Larsen. During the first few innings he was wild, but many of the Yankees, when they picked themselves out of the dirt at home plate, doubted that he was trying too hard to keep his control. In the third inning Larsen, whose temper was reaching the boiling point, made Harry Simpson duck away from a blazing fast ball. Both benches seemed on the point of going at each other and the Kansas City fans were demanding that the Athletics knock the stuffing out of the Bombers. The umpires held up the game and issued warnings to both benches.

Things seemed to settle down, but in the eighth inning Tom LaSorda, who had replaced Santiago, brushed Hank Bauer back with a pitch. A few seconds later Bauer hit the dirt when a wicked fast ball came straight for his head.

The Yankees came off the bench, screaming their protests, and Billy Martin's voice rose high above the others. Forgetting his good intentions, he laced it into LaSorda. He seemed about to run out to the mound when three Yankees pulled him back. Between pitches LaSorda glared angrily toward the fiery second baseman. When Mickey Mantle came up to hit, Billy cupped his hands over his mouth and screamed above the crowd's steady roar, "Knock him down and we'll chase you out of the park and into the river!"

LaSorda, about to pitch, suddenly slammed the ball down and strode toward the visitors' dugout. His eyes were blazing. It was a hot day in Kansas City, the temperature over ninety degrees. As he kept coming he hurled insults at Billy the Kid. "Come on!" he challenged. "I'll close up your big mouth!"

Billy, needing no urging, jumped out to meet the Athletic pitcher. The other Yankees followed him. From the dugout across the way stormed the Athletics, and Tom Flaherty, the umpire, hurriedly got between LaSorda and the raging second baseman. Billy's voice could be heard far up in the stands. "Let me get at him! He asked for it, Flaherty!"

Bill Summers moved in and got hold of Hank Bauer, and some of the Yankees helped the umpire calm the big ex-Marine down. Casey Stengel and four other players finally had Billy under control and the game was resumed.

The Kansas City fans behind the Yankee dugout, however, were not satisfied. They singled out Billy Martin for their target and labeled him everything short of a traitor to his country. When they asked him if he was still letting his wife and baby starve, he came out of the dugout and tried to get into the stands to swing on his tormentors. His teammates pulled him back. That night he was still raging.

"They boo a guy who tries to fight back!" he shouted. "They expect me to run and hide when LaSorda came after me? I'll fight back every time I know I'm right. I'll fight the Yankees if I have to. Ask them!"

By July 1st, Billy's batting average was below his usual average, but he was chosen as a member of the American League All-Star team and came up once as a pinch-hitter. During the five days that followed, he was side-lined by sacroiliac trouble, and he sweated and worried as he sat by and watched Bobby Richardson and Gil McDougald play in his place.

A man has to stay in there, even the old professionals, for sometimes it is hard to get back, especially when your replacement keeps hitting. Recently Phil Rizzuto had been released with what Yankee fans called a total lack of sentiment. They were still cool toward George Weiss. It told Billy only one thing. A baseball player's fortunes could change overnight.

On July 15th he was back in the line-up again; but a few days later Larry Doby, in a game against the

White Sox, knocked him over when he tried to complete a double play and he was badly shaken up. He
left the game and was out for three days. Then he
started hitting again, his average soaring to .286 by
August 1st. His spurt at the plate drew little attention,
for Mickey Mantle had become the center of interest
to baseball fans everywhere.

Mantle had hit forty-seven home runs. He was two
days ahead of Ruth's schedule the year the Babe hit
sixty circuit drives. Billy soon forgot his own troubles
in the excitement of urging Mantle on to break Ruth's
record.

Billy's average dropped to .267 by September 19th,
the day the Yankees clinched the 1956 pennant. As
usual he played a big part in a crucial game.

It was one of the greatest pitchers' battles of the
year, with Ford working against the White Sox ace,
Billy Pierce. Pierce had a 1-0 lead over the Yankees
going into the ninth and the first hitter to face him was
Billy Martin.

Mantle, in the batting circle, yelled, "Get hold of
one, Billy!"

"If you will," Billy threw back over his shoulder;
then, after a strike was called against him, he lashed
out at one of Pierce's fast balls and hit it deep to left.
He pulled up at third and shouted at Mantle, "All
right, you're next Mick!"

Mickey struck out, fired his bat away, and walked
back to the dugout, and Yogi Berra stepped in. Yogi
lifted a lazy fly that seemed a sure out, but Luis Aparicio, the White Sox shortstop and Minnie Minoso, the

third baseman, did a "you first" act and let it drop between them. Billy raced in to tie up the ball game.

The game went into extra innings, and it was Mickey Mantle who won it with a home run in the eleventh, making up for his strike-out in the ninth.

"You'll hear that hollering for somebody to break up the Yankees even louder now," Billy said as the jubilant Yankees peeled off their uniforms.

Mantle was the soberest of all the Yankees. His home runs had not been coming as often as he expected. His chance to beat the Babe's record seemed impossible now. "It's the walks they're giving me," he griped. "I wish a ten-foot bat was legal."

Billy laughed. "If I added my home runs to yours, you might make it."

As September ran out, stories were circulated blaming Billy for Mantle's failure to set a new home-run record. The Comet was even struggling for base hits. He was bad company for Mantle. He was keeping the slugger out late at night, after curfew, and leading him around to the taverns in all the American League cities.

"I'd deliberately hurt Mickey? Do you hurt a friend?" he lashed out at the writers. "All Mickey does is hit home runs and win triple-batting titles. Somebody hurt me like that!"

General manager George Weiss was not convinced. He sent word that Billy was to stop living at a hotel downtown and move into the Concourse-Plaza near the stadium, along with further instructions as to his behavior after working hours. Billy rebelled, considering that the Yankees did not own him to that extent.

One night he discovered that detectives were trailing him as he got out of a cab in front of the hotel. Once in his room, he poured out his resentment to Mantle. "They don't trust anybody. Now I know what Weiss thinks of me, and it won't matter what I've done for the ball club if he wants to cut me loose. Maybe if I'd gone into the used-car business or opened a scallopini restaurant when I was eighteen I'd be better off than I am now."

"You're kidding yourself," Mantle said, grinning. "You'd do the same thing all over again."

Billy grinned back and sat down on his bed. "Sure, I've had nice clothes. I've eaten well and I've been able to help my family have what other people have. The friends I've made — Mick, when I gripe like this again, hit me over the head."

Pre-World Series analysts troubled his mind again. Dodger sympathizers said Billy Martin was no longer a 154-game player. His old injuries were catching up with him. Hadn't Casey Stengel been juggling his line-up all year?

Casey Stengel laughed at the experts. "Sellin' that fella short again, are they? All right, he hits .264 for the year and fields .980, but when you throw a challenge at him you got to look out. Look back at his series record."

"I'll show them," Billy promised himself. "We'll get that championship back!"

Chapter XIV

OVER THIRTY-FOUR THOUSAND FANS packed Ebbets Field for the opening game of the World Series and, as was predicted, it was Whitey Ford opposing Sal Maglie.

Billy got one of the biggest thrills of his lifetime just before the game started. Along with several other Yankee stars, he was introduced to President Eisenhower by Casey Stengel. Afterward, along with the writers who were present, he claimed Old Case did it in his own particular brand of double-talk:

"And this is my fresh kid, and this is the big fella; this one is my professional, Mr. President, and this fella may blow a train but never a signal."

Actually he meant Billy Martin, Mickey Mantle, Whitey Ford, and Don Larsen, in that order.

Billy made good his threat to make his presence felt in the Bomber line-up. In the fourth inning he hit one of Maglie's pitches into the left-field seats for a home run, and he ribbed all the Dodger infielders as he circled the bases. When he reached the bench and started shaking hands, he grinned widely and said, "If I can hit the Barber, you guys can."

In the sixth the Brooklyn fans booed him to the skies when he called time and asked the umpire to examine the ball Maglie was throwing. It upset the Dodger pitcher for a few moments, but he went on to beat the Yankees, 6-2. When they asked Billy later if Maglie had been throwing illegal pitches, he grinned and shook his head.

"No, but you do everything to try and upset a pitcher going that good against you. I said to the umpire, 'Look, there's a spot on that ball. Pine tar, maybe.'" He laughed loudly. "Looks like I didn't rattle him enough. His curves are wicked, but next time we'll get him."

Both ball clubs arrived at the park the next afternoon and put on their uniforms, only to learn that the game was postponed. It had rained all morning; the skies were still overcast. Stengel told the writers he would shift his batting order around the next day. Skowron and Carey would be out, and Joe Collins would take over first base. Billy Martin would be shifted from second to third.

The bus taking the Yankees back across the river rumbled over the bridge. Fog hugged New York's tall buildings. Mantle and Billy agreed to relax in a movie and perhaps stop in at Harwyn's or Toots Shor's for a few minutes. They'd keep their minds occupied with anything but the Dodgers.

Whatever doubts Billy might have had just before the series had been driven into the stands with that ball he hit off Maglie. The determination to cross up his critics was even stronger after reading a telegram from Seventh Street in Berkeley which included the line: *"Here's a big kiss from Kelly Ann."* Out on the bay, at Al Faccini's place, his old friends would be watching every game on television. He had no intention of letting them down.

After an inning and a half of the second game the Brooklyn fans sat stunned. Big Don Newcombe, a twenty-seven-game winner in the National League, had been hammered for six hits and six runs. It looked like a typical Yankee rout, but the Dodgers came back in their half of the inning and tied the score. Bessent, Alston's relief pitcher, held the Yankees to two more runs. Shelling six other Yankee pitchers, the Dodgers added seven more runs and won, 13-8.

Billy Martin kicked things around in the gloomy Yankee dressing room. He had picked up but one hit. "We blow a six-run lead! I still can't believe it!"

Stengel, stung by the remarks of the working press, yelled at them, "You've got them fellers winning already. So we got to win four before they win two. We'll do it, because we've done it before!"

The Yankees were back in contention the next afternoon at the stadium, thanks to a great defensive play by none other than Billy Martin. When Brooklyn came to bat in the top of the ninth, the Yankees were leading, 5-3. But Dodger fans leaped to their feet and roared when Furillo led off with a solid smash to deep right field. Even as Billy watched Hank Bauer chase the ball, his mind was working swiftly. The Dodgers needed runs, with little time left. He had an idea that

Furillo would not hold up at second. Running out onto the grass, he yelled at Bauer to throw the ball to him.

Bauer's throw came in to him on a line. He whirled and saw Furillo streaking for third just as he suspected he would. His throw to Andy Carey had to be a perfect throw, and it was. Furillo dived into third on his stomach but was tagged out by a foot.

The play shook up the Dodgers. It choked off a rally, and the big stadium crowd rose up and gave Billy a deafening burst of applause. He grinned, looked up at the company box where George Weiss was sitting. So he was a bad influence on the Yankees!

"That throw of Billy's, his quick thinking, saved Ford's game," Stengel said in the clubhouse. "It could've saved the series. Supposin' that Furillo got to third, then scored on any kind of a hit. That means there's only one out and they're only a run behind. With them home-run hitters they got, it could have easily been tied up."

The Dodgers were leading by a run behind the pitching of their ace, Carl Erskine, when the Yankees came to bat in the bottom of the fourth inning. Mantle, first up, singled. When Berra struck out, Mantle stole second, and Enos Slaughter stepped up to hit. Billy picked a bat and waited in the on-deck circle.

The crowd booed when Alston ordered Slaughter walked in order to get at Billy Martin. Billy swung his head around and grinned at the Yankee bench. This was the way he liked it. And Casey Stengel made no move to put a long ball hitter in. In the parlance of athletes, the chips were down. The hitter he wanted was up there.

Erskine looked Billy over, coolly confident. He had stopped the pesky little player so far. He peered in and nodded at the sign from Campanella, and began throwing. Billy saw the pitch he liked coming in. He swung hard and drove it on a line to the outfield. Mantle scored to tie up the ball game. Slaughter scored a few minutes after on a sacrifice fly and the Yankees forged ahead. Sturdivant went on to check the Dodgers and won it, 6-2. The series was all even.

"Of course I didn't consider Alston's move an insult," Billy said in the clubhouse. "After all, who wouldn't walk a hitter like Slaughter who had a series average of .900 when he came up to bat? To get at a two-sixty hitter like me. But if that's Dodger strategy, I hope they stay with it."

At the end of the eighth inning of the fifth contest, the tension in Yankee Stadium was almost unbearable. The Yankees led, 2-0. The Dodgers had no runs and not a single hit. Don Larsen had not even allowed a Dodger to reach first base. When he faced the Dodgers in the first of the ninth, the only sound in the big ball park seemed to be the high-pitched voice of Billy Martin. Larsen got the first two men easily and then Alston sent Dale Mitchell in to pinch-hit.

Billy prayed a ball would not be hit his way. The player who spoiled this performance would never forget it as long as he lived. When Dale Mitchell looked at a called third strike to end the history-making game,

Billy raced in to throw his arms around Larsen.

Before turning in that night, Billy said to Mantle, "Next year I'm going to bring my whole family to see a World Series. They never saw me play, Mick. Even my little kid, Kelly Ann will be here. I'll be over thirty then, and maybe it will be my last."

"How old is Enos Slaughter?" Mantle asked him. "Billy, something's bothering you again."

"I get hurt a lot, Mick. I've got that leg muscle I keep dipping into the whirlpool bath, but it keeps nagging at me. And don't forget George Weiss. He never liked me much. He and Case, I keep hearing, have arguments about me."

He had a hard time getting to sleep. Had he only imagined lately that Old Case had not been as friendly toward him as he used to be? Stengel used to grin when he'd rib him about the oil wells and banks he owned. Only a few days ago he'd asked Case if he figured to build another bank just to keep his World Series winnings in, and Stengel had seemed a little touchy about it. But he had to put his worries aside. He had to be in shape tomorrow.

Clem Labine shut the Yankees out, 1-0, in the sixth game, allowing just four hits. Billy got one of them.

Yogi Berra was solemn in the clubhouse. Out in St. Louis, his mother had suffered the amputation of her right arm. Worry had silenced his big bat against Labine. Billy went over to him and asked him about his mother.

"I called last night and asked what I could do for

her. She said get her a couple of home runs. Tomorrow I'll do that, Billy."

"Keep thinking that," Billy said. "You will."

In the seventh and deciding game Alston started Newcombe again. Johnny Kucks would go for the Yankees. Stengel shook up his batting order, putting Billy in the number-two position. Hank Bauer hit a single to start the ball game off, but Billy struck out. Mickey Mantle also struck out. Yogi Berra stepped in and waved his big bat at Newcombe. With two strikes against him he drove the ball over the barrier in right field.

"That's the first one, Yog," Billy said when the Yanks rose up to welcome Berra back to the dugout. "Didn't I say you would?"

With one out, Billy hit a single off Newcombe in the third, but Mantle went down swinging again. The crowd roared with glee, certain that Newcombe would go on to stop the Bombers. But then the skies darkened over Flatbush. Yogi Berra came up and drove the ball out into Bedford Avenue again and the Yankees were out in front, 4-0.

"You got 'em for her, Yog!" Billy shouted when Berra sat down on the bench. "I sure would like to see the smile on her face."

Walter Alston stayed with Newcombe, but in the top of the fourth, Elston Howard drove another home run into the left-field seats. The Dodger manager came out, and soon Newcombe shuffled off the diamond, head bent, a picture of dejection. The Brooklyn crowd booed him. On the bench, Billy said angrily, "Listen to that! This crowd didn't deserve the pennant."

Inning after inning, Kucks silenced the Brooklyn bats. Billy got his second hit of the game in the sixth. Mantle walked, and Alston ordered his pitcher to throw four wide ones to Berra to load the bases. He'd gamble by having Skowron pitched to. Skowron hit a grand-slam home run, and Dodger fans began heading for the exits. It was 9-0, Yankees. Ebbets Field was as quiet as a tomb.

Brooklyn failed to get a run off Kucks, and the Yankees were champions of the world once more. Billy walked into the jam-packed visitors' dressing room with a batting average of .296 for the seven games. He had fielded to perfection. When the refreshments were broken out, the Yankee executives, Weiss, Topping, and Webb came in. They shook hands with all the players and told them what a great job they had done.

When Billy shook hands with Weiss, the big man seemed a little embarrassed. Perhaps, Billy thought, he'll feel different about me next year. After this series he saw no reason why he would not be solidly entrenched in the Yankee organization. During the winter months he'd get a lot of rest and give that leg muscle a chance to fully heal. He felt that 1957 would be one of his best years.

On his way to the coast, the excitement over, the winning shares counted and split, Billy suddenly wondered why he wasn't the happiest and luckiest man in the world. Why did he have to turn to cold, hard facts? Weiss and the others would already be looking toward 1957, he told himself. Weaknesses in the Yankee line-up would be discussed and the necessary measures taken. Personal feelings went down the drain. Past performances meant nothing. He looked back to that day that seemed so long ago, when he met Casey Stengel for the first time. His mood changed and he smiled to himself. He was certain he could depend on Old Case.

Back in Berkeley, he ordered more improvements on the two-story house. "So much you have done already, Billy. So little we ever did for you?" his mother said.

"Too much?" Billy asked and forced a laugh. "Remember I let you all starve while I drove big automobiles? People fool you. They shake hands with me on the street and say what a great ballplayer I am, but I know what a lot of them are thinking. They would love to see me hit the skids, Mama."

"All this you imagine, Billy. It is not good to think like that."

Billy nodded. "You are right. You and Nona were always right. I think I'll go down to Al Faccini's and see if I can meet some of the old gang. You have a big steak ready for me. No vegetables, remember!"

He did not reach Faccini's. He came to an all-too-familiar vacant lot a block from Seventh Street where a bunch of kids were playing ball. It was late October, football weather, but kids in the San Francisco Bay area seldom put their bats or gloves away. A voice in the process of changing yelled, "It's Billy Martin!" and the game broke up and he was surrounded. He answered all their questions and gave them tips on how to hold a bat. He spent a few minutes hitting grounders to them.

One little fellow suddenly ran off the lot as if a ferocious bear was after him. A freckled-faced kid laughed and said, "Tony's always late for choir practice."

Memories swept in and over the Yankee infielder. That was little Billy Martin running lickety-split toward St. Ambrose's. There would be many more like him. They were the future Rizzutos and DiMaggios, the Gehrigs and the Musials.

Chapter XV

HE SPENT AS MUCH TIME as he was allowed with his little daughter, Kelly Ann. He brought her toys enough to start a store. Holding her, he would say, "Cute. Sweeter than a homer with the bases loaded. Nona would say, 'Bellino' if she could be here. Someday I'll tell you about her."

At times like these he became fully aware of his responsibilities, and knew he needed at least three more years with the Yankees. Two more World Series shares were not more than he should expect, for most of the other American League teams were in the process of rebuilding. He'd have to struggle along physically at times, but he knew other players who had kept going with worse miseries plaguing them. Like Mickey Mantle, his roommate.

Billy had seen Mantle carry on despite a bad knee; he had seen the Comet's face twist with pain when he swung at a fast ball and missed. Mantle had overcome a case of osteomylitis when he was in his teens. He shouldn't let himself forget there were ballplayers with as many problems as he had, perhaps more.

146

He shunned all unnecessary physical activity during the winter and took treatments for his back. He was among the early birds at St. Petersburg in March, 1957, determined to be in the best shape possible by opening day of another pennant race. He noticed no great change in Stengel's attitude toward him, even though the manager kept him on the bench during the early exhibition games. He knew the reason for it: Casey wanted a good look at Richardson and Tony Kubek. He played a few innings against the St. Louis Cardinals on March 16th and his legs felt good under him. He did not see real action until eleven days later when, for the first time, he became aware that Stengel's paternal interest in him had begun to cool.

He had a sore throat and a slight fever. Stengel came out of his office with some writers and called to him, "Billy, can you play today?"

"Sure, Case," he said, and then he heard Stengel say to the scribes as he walked off, "Some of them better be. They been watching that Kubek and that fella, Richardson. The way them two fellas are going, they should be scared."

He played his best that day and yelled as loudly as ever, despite his ailing throat, but he resented Stengel's insinuation that a lot of his veterans were dogging it, including his second baseman. It was a bitter pill to swallow, for never in his life had he played the game of baseball without exerting every last ounce of his ability. It seemed certain now that Weiss intended to win an argument with Casey Stengel and he would have to watch every move he made. He was thoroughly convinced of it when George Weiss summoned him to his office a few days later. When he walked in, Weiss eyed him closely. Billy was puzzled, for he had not been on anything but his best behavior. In at twelve every night, things like that. "You sent for me, Mr. Weiss," he said.

Weiss picked up some papers, then laid them down again. Out of the blue he snapped, "I hate to tell you this, Martin, but you get into any trouble and we'll do something drastic."

Billy stared at the man, fighting his temper. There was no justification for this kind of talk. "You have nothing to worry about, Mr. Weiss. Trouble is the last thing I'm looking for."

"You've been warned, Martin," Weiss said and turned back to his work.

Billy immediately sought out Stengel. "He had no reason to say that to me, Case," he complained bitterly. "Why is he singling me out? I've tried to get along with Mr. Weiss, and never had anything against him. Why, I wrote letters to him during the winters. I've done everything but lick his boots. Why doesn't he like me?"

Stengel failed to come up with an answer and even seemed to be hedging. A little sick at heart, Billy left Stengel's suite at the Soreno, wondering how they expected a player to do his best under such conditions.

The Yankees looked like anything but a champion-

ship club during the first three weeks of the 1957 season. The Chicago White Sox took the play away from
them. Billy was being shifted between second and
third base and his hitting was feeble. It seemed certain
he would be benched until the Yankees met the Senators on the 24th. He stayed in the line-up despite a
severely bruised wrist sustained two days before. The
Yankees lost, 3-1, but he made four hits and batted in
the only Bomber run in the third.

The Yankees played a ragged defensive game. The
rookie Kubek lost Berberet's long fly in the sun in the
eighth and Jim Lemon, who had singled, eventually
scored. Roy Sievers won it in the ninth with a two-run
homer. Joe Trimble of the *Daily News* wrote that the
only Yankee who played like a Yankee was Billy Martin.

Stengel was no ray of sunshine in the dressing room:
"I'll go along with this line-up for a while, but some of
you fellas better start hustling or you'll figure in a trade
before the deadline."

The writers dropped Billy a question out of earshot
of Stengel. "We still hear they're going to break you
and Mantle up."

"I hear they're getting ready to fly to the moon,"
Billy said. "They do that and Mick and me will just
keep two other guys out late."

On the night of May 15th, Whitey Ford and Mickey
Mantle told Billy they had arranged a birthday celebration for him at the Copacabana in New York. "We're
bringing our wives, so wear a necktie," Whitey said.

"Hank Bauer, Kucks, and Yogi are coming along."

"How about it?" Mantle said. "You're only twenty-nine once, Billy."

"If you don't hand me the tab when it's over."

The party ran smoothly until two-twenty in the morning. At the table next to the Yankees was a party of seventeen people, a bowling team out celebrating. They became noisy and got a little out of hand. Once Billy heard a remark he was certain was directed toward him, but he let it pass. One of the bowlers got up and came near the Yankees' table. He said something that angered Hank Bauer.

A bouncer moved in and said to Bauer, "Don't fool around with those guys. We'll take care of them." Almost before Billy was aware of it, Bauer was over near the employees' locker room, and Berra and Kucks were pinning his arms.

"Come on, let's get out of here," Billy said and quickly left the table. On the way to the hotel in a cab with Mantle, Whitey, and Mrs. Ford, he had misgivings. If too much publicity came of this, he knew he would bear the burden of guilt. Reporters would twist the facts to suit themselves.

"There were a lot of witnesses there," Mantle assured him. "They'll speak up if they have to."

"I'm Billy Martin, remember?" the second baseman retorted.

As he had feared, the newspapers made the most they could out of the incident. A man named Edward Jones claimed Hank Bauer had struck him and threat-

ened to sue the Yankee outfielder. Bauer denied the
charge, and customers of the Copa, when questioned,
could not be certain about what really happened.

George Weiss and Casey Stengel acted quickly.
Heavy fines were imposed on the players involved, and
Whitey Ford, who was to be the starting pitcher on
May 17th, was withdrawn. Yogi Berra was benched.

The Yankees got worse. By June 15th they trailed
the White Sox by five games, and for the preceding
three weeks Billy took the brunt of the ridicule thrown
at the Bombers by the fans and opposing benches.
"The Copa Kid!" they yelled at him. Old Case no longer laughed and slapped his knee when Billy came up
with a choice remark about an opposing player or umpire. Something big, he heard from every side, was
brewing in the Yankee front office. His hitting was
feeble. His average was .241 on June 15th when the
Yankees lost to the White Sox, 7-6, at Comiskey Park.
He got two hits out of three trips to the plate against
Harshman and Keegan, and hoped his luck had turned.

The deal that shook the baseball world was made on
June 15th, 1957. The Yankees traded Billy Martin to
the Kansas City Athletics for Harry Simpson. Yankee
players Terry, Martyn, and Woody Held were also
given up by the Bombers. Billy Martin was informed
he was no longer a Yankee during the sixth inning of
the game between the Yankees and Athletics in Kansas City on June 16th. He played the rest of the game
as if in his sleep, and when he reached the Yankee
dressing room, he said with tears in his eyes, "Gosh, I

hate to leave this club, but trading is a part of the game. I knew it was coming."

The other Bombers could not believe it. Whitey Ford sat down in front of his locker and stared at the floor.

"It's like losing a brother," Mantle said to the writers crowding the room. "He's the best friend I ever had."

Billy took off his uniform and stared at the Yankee insignia on the front of the shirt. He knew he'd never wear it again. He tried to hold back the lump that came up in his throat. George Weiss had finally had his way.

In the bus taking the players to their hotel, Enos Slaughter said, "Somebody must be crazy."

Billy sat next to Bobby Richardson, heir to his job with the Yankees. Richardson gave Billy his hand. "Good luck, Kid," he said.

The bus merged with downtown traffic. Billy felt as if he had been jabbed with a million needles. His thinking at the moment was numbed. No more World Series shares. He was going to a ball club heading for nowhere. But the thing that cut him deepest was the snipping of the cord of sentiment that had held Casey Stengel and him together since the day Red Adams brought him into the Oakland ball park.

He felt certain that Stengel could have prevented the deal if he had really been set against it. It was apparent that Old Case wanted him to go. His desire to stay in the good graces of George Weiss was stronger than loyalty. Yes, baseball at times could be a hard and cold business.

To break the tension Whitey Ford said, "When you

hit against me, Billy, I'll sometimes have to brush you back."

"Do that," Billy said forcing a grin, "and your kids won't get any more Christmas presents."

One thing he was determined to do as always. He would play his heart out for Kansas City, especially when they met the Yankees.

He packed up and said his good-byes as quickly as he could. Writers waylaid him in the lobby of the hotel and he threw at them, "I've nothing to say. Ask Stengel. He has all the answers."

He would dread returning to New York. It was his town. He had made a lot of friends there.

Lou Boudreau welcomed him to the Kansas City clubhouse the next afternoon and assured him that he would be treated right. "The stands out there are almost packed, Billy. They like the deal."

"Sure," Billy said. The Athletic uniform seemed too small for him. It stirred memories of hand-me-downs he had to accept when he was a small kid. "They're pitching Johnny Kucks today, Lou," he said. "I'll hit him good."

Leading off in the fourth inning, he rapped Kucks for a single and the crowd gave him a big round of applause as he took his lead-off first. Noren hit a long drive that Mantle caught, and Cerv popped up. Lou Skizas lifted a short fly to left where Yogi Berra was playing that day, and the catcher, unused to the outfield, did not break in quickly enough. Billy raced in to score.

He sparkled in the field, making two plays that put an end to threatened Yankee uprisings. In the eighth, with the score tied, he came up and hit a home run that put Kansas City ahead, 3-2.

Hollering it up in the infield, he hoped the one-run lead would stand up. It would mean that a player the Yankees had traded the day before had beaten them. It would be embarrassing to the Yankee front office. But it didn't happen. Elston Howard drove in the winning runs in the ninth for the Yankees and won it, 4-3.

Billy got two hits in five times at bat, had scored all three runs for the Athletics. Kansas City fans left the park, positive that their club had gotten the better of the deal.

Three days later, against Washington, Billy slugged out three hits, including a double and a home run off Kemmerer. But even his presence could not keep a fire burning under the indifferent Athletics. They began to fade, and by June 29th they had dropped eight straight games and were sixteen and a half games behind. Old injuries slowed Billy down and he spent much of his time on the bench. Boudreau, pressed for a strong inner defense, asked him to play when his legs could hardly hold him up. "We'll make it up to you in money, Billy," Boudreau promised.

Martin went out there and tried to forget the pain along with the heartbreak he brought with him to the Athletics.

His batting fell off. The Kansas City fans began to ride him hard. They advised him to go back to the

Copa, for they were sure he could play much better there. The enemy bench jockeys took up the cry. He was a has-been, a playboy.

Vainly but untiringly he tried to lift the morale of the Kansas City players. His deepest worry was that their "Who cares?" attitude would brush off on him. He knew that nothing worse could happen to a ballplayer. One day, in a game against the Baltimore Orioles, he ran in to give encouragement to one of Boudreau's relief pitchers. The hurler eyed him with amusement and said, "What are you gettin' excited about? We ain't goin' anywhere."

It made him a little sick. He felt like running to the bench and yelling at Boudreau, "Get that quitter out of there!"

Instead, he said, grinning, "All right, throw it, then duck. I hope it hits you in the head." He ran back to his position, banged his fist into his glove, and yelled, "Let's g-g-g-g-go! Let's get 'em!"

Willie Miranda, Paul Richards' fine fielding shortstop was on second, and Billy Gardner was on first. Boyd, a good hitter, was up there, and the Orioles needed one run to tie up the ball game.

If the relief pitcher did not get by the hard-hitting first baseman, they had the dangerous Francona to contend with. And then Gus Triandos. Boyd fouled the first two pitches off, and then waited out Boudreau's left-hander. He ran the count to three balls and two strikes, and then swung hard at a fast ball.

Boyd connected solidly. Miranda, with two out, had

started running with the pitch. But Billy had been watching Boyd's feet just before that pitch went in. The batter had shifted his feet and Billy was heading for the hole between first and short, even as the rifle crack of the bat lifted the fans to their feet. Running at top speed, he made a stab for the ball as it hit the grass just over the dirt of the infield, and got it in the palm of his glove. Off-balance he fired a throw to first that got Boyd by half a step.

In a World Series it would have been called a miraculous play.

Billy kept his eyes away from Boudreau's pitcher when he settled down on the bench. The man did not deserve to win this game, but he'd do *his* best to win it for him.

George Kell tied the game in the seventh with a triple, driving in Brideweser, the former Yankee second baseman, who had walked and been sacrificed to second.

In the eighth Hector Lopez doubled off Billy Loes. With two out, Billy Martin stepped up and he grinned as Gus Triandos asked him if he ever got that fine back they had plastered on him after that night-club incident in New York.

"It's a hot day, Gus," he said. "I think I'll end this. I don't feel like extra innings." He hit Loes' second pitch and drove Lopez in. It was 3-2, Kansas City, when the last out was made.

Chapter XVI

THE ATHLETICS went from bad to worse and the fans demanded Boudreau's scalp, and got it. Harry Craft, a Kansas City coach, and once a Cincinnati Reds outfielder, was given the job. A few days later he made a statement that angered Billy and the other ex-Yankees on the club, although they had to admit there was some truth in it.

"All Yankees require careful handling," Craft said. "They all feel sorry for themselves for at least a year after they have been let go. Then they realize they have to eat and settle down to real work."

"In a way he's right," Billy Martin told the writers. "You get used to winning and you like it. I get mad when the Athletics lose. I try to tell them they can win, but they laugh at me. Don't forget, you can't build a fire under anything if you haven't kindling wood to start with."

He got a big measure of satisfaction out of beating the Yankees on August 22nd, 6-3. It was the day Kansas City climbed out of the cellar and won the first series from the Yankees since 1955. Billy played third that day and batted in sixth position.

From the moment Johnny Kucks stepped to the pitching mound, Billy tormented him from the dugout steps. Vic Power started it off hitting a single. Kucks hit Hunter with a pitch, and Bob Cerv singled after big Gus Zernial flied out. The bases were full.

In the batter's circle, Billy yelled, "How late were you out last night, Johnny?"

Kucks yelled something in at Billy, then pitched to Woody Held. Held smashed a single and drove in two runs.

Billy stepped into the batter's box and grinned out at Kucks. After a called strike he thought was in too close, he stepped out and got dirt on his hands. He glanced toward the Yankee dugout and saw Stengel waving to the bullpen and wondered what Old Case's thoughts were.

Kucks threw one in that hit Billy on the left hand. Running down to first to load the bases again, he yelled at Kucks, "You wouldn't do that on purpose, would you, Johnny?"

Stengel walked out to the mound, and while the game waited until a relief pitcher came in, Billy tried to catch the manager's eye, but Old Case looked everywhere but in his direction.

"Have a nice shower," Billy shouted as Kucks left the mound.

The Athletics scored three runs in the inning and were never headed. They had taken eleven out of sixteen since Craft took over.

When the Athletics came to the stadium he felt

homesick for the Yankee clubhouse. It would be foolish for him to deny that he still felt a deep resentment
toward the Yankee officials who had traded him away
and that Casey Stengel was no longer his idol. The
first thing he did when he arrived at the big ball park
was to stop at a stand and buy some fruit for the elder-
ly woman who ran the switchboard for the Yankees.
He had always done this.

"You never forget, do you?" the woman said, beam-
ing. "How is my Billy Martin?"

"I'll bet you say that to all the boys," he laughed, and
his heart felt much lighter as he made his way to the
visitors' dressing room.

The Yankees were pitching Whitey Ford, his old
pal, today. A hit or two off Whitey would sure be good
for a lot of things ailing him. In the dressing room he
began to steam the Athletics up if only for his own
state of mind. He had a "book" on all Stengel's hitters.
He kept reminding the pitchers of Yankee weaknesses.
"Look out for that Berra," he said. "When you're up
there hitting he'll watch your feet and then signal to
the fielders. But you can decoy him."

The Yankees thumped the A's, but Billy had an en-
joyable afternoon. In the fifth Mantle hit a sharp
grounder his way and he dug it out of the dirt and
hesitated. He let Mickey run full tilt for first base, then
fired the ball to Vic Power at the last second to get
Mantle by a step. His shrill voice, he knew, must be
jarring Old Case's ears as he kept up an incessant verbal attack against his old teammates. In the seventh he

drove a ball deep to the left-field seats for a home run, and his face wore a delighted grin as he trotted around the bases. The New York fans who would never forget him applauded him as he ran to the Athletic dugout.

Injuries benched him two days later. He was glad he sat in the dugout as he watched the Red Sox crush the Athletics, 16-0. As the days passed, his inactivity began to get under the skins of Kansas City fans. Reports were circulated that he was not giving his best to Harry Craft and that his injuries were not serious enough to keep him out of the line-up. They said he was playing all right in the night clubs.

One night when he came in late from a movie in Cleveland, he suspected that Craft was keeping a check on him. He lost no time seeking out the manager after breakfast the next morning.

"I thought I was through with that stuff when I left the Yankees, Harry!" he snapped. "Look, it isn't my fault the way this club is going."

"I never said it was, Billy. Don't believe all you hear."

"I guess I shouldn't," he shot back. "Like the promise they made me when I joined this ball club. I've never seen that extra money Boudreau promised me."

"When Lou left," Craft said, "All the promises he made went with him. You should have pinned him down before he left."

"Parke Carroll, the business manager, knew it," Billy argued. "I wish you'd take it up with him."

"I'll do that," Craft said, "but he's not a man to throw money around."

"Say," Billy suddenly asked, "Wasn't he with the Yankee organization once?"

Craft nodded.

"Then it figures," Billy said. "I'll have to sing for that money and I'm no Eddie Fisher."

His injuries healed, Billy took over at his old position the last of August and got a single out of three trips against Alex Kellner in a 3-1 defeat of the White Sox. His great stop of a ball hit to his right by Minnie Minoso convinced thousands of fans that he was holding nothing back for Kansas City even though they were hopelessly out of the race.

He was hitting .268 going into September, but old miseries came back to slow him down and he was out of action most of the time. He finished the season with an unimpressive .251, and baseball experts all over the country intimated that the Yankees had made no mistake when they had traded Billy Martin. In their estimation he was a step slower in the infield although he had fielded .982. He could not expect his loud voice to make up for his light hitting much longer. Allowances were made for him, however. Being dropped from the top of the league to the bottom could discourage even the greatest player and reduce his efficiency. Another year like 1957 could be his downfall.

They could be right, Billy admitted. A fiery, competitive spirit could die in the humdrum of a consistent loser. But he refused to accept such a possibility, for even a man sent to the salt mines of Siberia had a chance to get out of them. Starting from scratch in the spring, he might build the fire under the Athletics. Perhaps some good trades during the winter would bring the right players to Kansas City. Meanwhile, as his grandmother always said, some prayers would help.

When the Yankees lost to the Milwaukee Braves in the World Series, the writers came up with some alibis for Stengel that took five years off Billy's age. The Yankees had been unable to come up with that key hit against Lew Burdette, for their great series clutch player had been with Kansas City. To prove their point, they reviewed past series games the Yankees could have lost if Billy Martin had not been with them.

"That'll kind of burn George Weiss and Old Case," Billy said in Al Faccini's place in Berkeley. "You know something? A guy like Frank Lary beats them four times during a season and they call him a Yankee tamer. Burdette beats them three times in seven games. I think they're ready to be taken."

He received many offers of speaking engagements but turned them down. Lacking a fat World Series check that year, he had to go out and make some money. "After all, I've said all I've got to say about Stengel and the Yankees," he explained. He accepted a job with a Kansas City firm as an automobile salesman and proved highly successful.

In November of 1957, Detroit's general manager, Johnny McHale, contacted the Kansas City front office and asked how much they would have to give up to get the Athletics shortstop, Joe DeMaestri.

"DeMaestri?" came the reply. "Do you want Billy Martin?"

"Are you serious?" McHale asked.

The Athletics' front office was. McHale did not hesitate. He gave up the players Kansas City demanded, and closed the deal before the other American League clubs could get a bid in. Every club, with the exception of the Yankees, made offers when it was learned Billy Martin was for sale. They were all too late.

Billy could scarcely believe his ears when McHale called him on the phone. His contract called for more money than even the Yankees had paid him. His pride and confidence flamed brighter than ever, especially when he learned that every manager in the league outside of Stengel had wanted him. All his small doubts and nagging fears vanished. In a few weeks he would be on his way to Lakeland, Florida, the training camp of the Detroit Tigers. It was a great ball club, a real contender.

"We needed a natural leader, a take-charge guy," Jack Tighe, the Tigers manager said. "Sure, Billy is a .261 hitter, but that average is misleading. His winning spirit is only one of his intangible assets. He'll fight you right down to the wire if no more than five bucks is at stake. He'll be our shortstop."

"How about Harvey Kuenn?" Tighe was asked.

"I'm going to make an outfielder out of him," he told the skeptics.

When Billy arrived in New York just after the winter baseball meetings on his way to Buffalo where he was to speak at a March of Dimes Dinner, the writers waylaid him in the hotel.

"Charlie Dressen," one said, "claims you can't make the throw from short, Billy."

He laughed. "Dressen has a short memory. I played shortstop for him in Oakland and he never complained. I've got a good arm. Once I played an inning for Joe DiMaggio in centerfield. All right, it'll take a lot of work. Fielding the ball will be no trouble. The trick is to get into position to throw the ball, to have enough on the throw to complete the double plays. At second you fire the ball across your body, but at short you have to throw straight and then get out of the way of the runner. They run right down your throat."

He caught them studying him and knew they were seeing the little crow's feet around his eyes and the slight trace of wrinkles around his mouth. It was as if they were measuring the time he had left and they seemed a little sad.

"Sorry, but I have to go," Billy told them. "You'll be knocking me for at least another five years. Remember, I've stopped looking for trouble." He laughed loudly and walked away. A few moments later he looked at himself in the mirror. He saw a man who'd had a job done on his nose so that he would be a little more pleasant to look at. He noticed a more important change in his eyes. A lot of the old beligerence had gone out of them. There was a better way, he knew now, to overcome an obstacle without hitting out at it with your fists.

That is, of course, if what was in your way did not hit you first. He had to laugh, for he was always honest with himself.

Chapter XVII

THE DETROIT PLAYERS, training at Lakeland, Florida, welcomed Billy warmly, but underneath the surface of the Tigers he read traces of resentment. He did not blame them for this. The newspapers said part of his job with Tighe would be to build a fire under them. During the winter the Detroit front office had struck a match in the form of salary cuts and many of the big Detroit stars were already burning.

After the initial workouts that took the winter rust out of muscles and joints, Tighe got down to serious business, tackling his first big problem of converting Kuenn into a centerfielder and making Billy Martin his shortstop.

"You know about Kuenn, Billy. He's got too much weight now to play short. He's always played around the middle of the diamond and likes a direct look at the ball coming his way. He'll get that in center. He can still run fast straight ahead."

"Just play me where you want to every day, Jack," Billy said. "I don't care much where."

Tighe called over a man who had been hitting ground balls to the Tiger infielders. He had patches of silver at his temples and a crackling of wrinkles around his eyes. "Billy, you know Johnny Pesky. I'm putting him in charge of you."

Billy knew he'd never have a better teacher. Pesky had been with the great Red Sox team of 1946 that won the pennant, and had played both third and short. He got right down to work with Pesky, who showed him the best way to come in on ground balls hit toward shortstop, and kept reminding him he'd have to kind of circle around to get some of them. The ex-Red Sox player soon found out there was nothing wrong with Billy's arm.

It wasn't easy at first. He made mistakes but never the same one twice. He doggedly hung in there, his only fear being that one of the fast breaks from short would injure that balky thigh muscle again.

Tighe, just before the exhibition games, threw two teams against each other. Billy, in the midst of a bunch of rookies, had a chance to stop drives by hitters like Kaline, Maxwell, Kuenn, and Boone. They deliberately attempted to smash them his way. In the third inning with Bolling on first, Boone slammed one to his right that looked headed for the outfield, but he back-handed the ball and threw to first off-balance. The ball sailed three feet over the first baseman's head.

"Anything wrong with his arm?" Jack Tighe asked the coaches sitting on the bench with him.

Pesky grinned all over his face as he watched Billy make the plays a shortstop had to make. "You can stop worrying about him, Jack," he said. "Kuenn is the only question mark now."

In the Detroit clubhouse, at the hotel, Billy was a source of merriment. He told about the days he acted as a hunting dog for his stepfather out at Point Isabelle and the escapades of his bush-league days. How he drove Mantle crazy when the Yankee slugger tried to teach him how to rope a cow. Jack Tighe was sure Detroit had found what it needed most. He knew his own job was being made easy by Billy Martin. He had a rookie named Reno Bertoia trying out at third. The kid had a lot to learn. When Billy played next to Bertoia he would talk with him about situations on the diamond as they presented themselves, and tell him how to play certain batters. He soon had the rookie relaxed and full of confidence.

His legs feeling good under him, Billy went about doing what was expected of him. He used his voice on veteran and rookie alike. One day after the hitters had looked bad in a game with their farm club, Charleston, he yelled at them, "You remind me of the White Sox. How can you win games when you need four singles to score one run?"

The Tigers, when he got on them a little too hard, had a way of calming him down. They would ask him what he heard from Stengel. He was always more hurt than angry at these moments. Once he yelled at Kaline and Maxwell, "He had to do what he did or Weiss would have fired him too." A big grin swept over his face. "He's not too well off you know." No longer a Yankee, he had some opinions about some of his old teammates.

"Some of them do have heads too big for their hats,"

he said. "One or two of them always wondered why a Dago like me wanted better things than I had when I left Seventh Street out in Berkeley. I wasn't supposed to have an opinion of my own."

Jack Tighe thoroughly enjoyed this kind of talk. His team had always been rough on the Yankees. This year, with Billy, they should be much rougher.

Billy played a strong game at shortstop during the exhibition games, and when Detroit moved north, the experiment with Harvey Kuenn as an outfielder seemed to have succeeded. In his hotel room, the night before opening day of the 1958 pennant race, he began to realize that too much might be expected of him. Even though he had a dismal season with Kansas City, Detroit fans expected him to be the difference between a team that had finished twenty games behind the Yankees in 1957 and a pennant winner. They expected him to work magic.

Detroit fans had read that he had led the Tigers in singing on the long bus rides to and from grapefruit-league games. He had made the shyest players on Tighe's bench expert bench jockeys, and had them believing they could win the pennant if they kept thinking they could.

Billy hoped he could live up to half of what was expected of him.

The first few weeks of the pennant race became a nightmare to him. They had him walking the floor at night. The Tigers could not seem to win. Hitters like Boone, Kaline, and Kuenn could hardly buy an extra base hit. The vaunted pitching staff led by Frank Lary and Jim Bunning could not get started. The disgruntled fans in Detroit picked Billy out as their whipping boy. After all, hadn't McHale bought him to make this team go?

Cleveland was in Briggs Stadium one afternoon and the Tigers were leading 4-1 when Billy came up to bat in the sixth. McLish threw a strike past him that looked wide of the plate and he protested to the plate umpire.

"Knock it off, Martin!" a leather-lunged fan yelled. "You're not with the Yankees now."

When he struck out for the second time, even a Detroit writer yelled at him from the press box, "We had that much last year!"

"Go back to Kansas City!" a fan hollered at him when he ran to the mound in the eighth to talk to Tighe's relief pitcher.

The abuse stung him deep, but he quickly shook it off. He could not blame the crowd; they had a right to expect better baseball from the Tigers. They seemed to forget he was hitting .290 for Detroit this early in June, and he was playing a steady game at shortstop.

The Yankees kept winning and the Tigers kept losing. Detroit was out of first place by ten and a half games by July 2nd. Miss Billy Martin? New York fans no longer questioned George Weiss' judgment.

"We'll get going," Billy kept saying, "wait and see."

Dwindling gate receipts convinced the Detroit owners early in June they had gone far enough with Jack Tighe. They let him go and brought in Bill Norman, manager of their Charleston club in the American Association. Norman, they felt sure, would rule with an iron hand; Tighe had been too easy with the temperamental Detroit stars. The Tigers were in Boston when the change was made.

"Jack took the rap," Billy Martin told the writers, "but the hired hands are to blame. They aren't playing as well as they know how. I can't understand it."

The new broom began to sweep cleaner. The Tigers began an upsurge, and when they visited the stadium in New York they were out of the cellar. They beat the Bombers, 4-2, belting Shantz and Grim for nine hits, and afterward, in the visitors' side of the clubhouse, Billy ran around, yelling, "It's great to be a winner, isn't it? The Yanks win because they have that feeling."

"Think it will be this way the rest of the year?" an outfielder asked him, a dubious look on his face.

Beating the Yanks were red-letter days for Billy Martin. The Bombers came to Detroit several days later and ran into Frank Lary again. Nearly thirty thousand fans were in Briggs Stadium on this Saturday afternoon, and they screamed with delight as inning after inning went by without a Yankee getting across the plate.

In the second inning McDougald got a single but died on first base. Mickey Mantle got hit by a pitch in the fourth but got nowhere when Billy Martin stopped a smash off Carey's bat and got the third out. Kaline came up in the Tiger half and slammed Duke Maas' pitch into the right-field seats for a home run.

Billy hooted at the Yankees all through the game, and in the sixth he really got his chance to taunt them.

With runners on first and second and only one out, Lary fanned Kubek. Mantle came to bat and singled to right, and Duke Maas, the runner on second, was waved around third by the Yankee coach, Crosetti. Billy could hardly believe it, for the ball had been hit out to Kaline in a hurry, and Al had one of the strongest arms in the league.

Billy did not run out onto the grass because he knew there would be no relay. Kaline threw a strike to Red Wilson, his catcher, and nailed Maas by at least three feet.

"You tell the Crow he's getting old, Mick!" Billy shouted at Mantle as the Yankee slugger headed for his position in centerfield. "That was some boner and it could cost you the ball game."

Detroit won the game, 1-0, their eighth win in eleven games against New York. They were only eight and a half games out of first place and the Detroit fans, pouring out of the park, were talking about a pennant.

"You were ribbing Mantle," Jim Bunning said to Billy afterward. "About his .283 batting average?"

"I'm not that crazy. He'll be hitting over three hundred before long and he could hurt us." He grinned and shook his head. "You know, I'm meeting him later. A fine thing, isn't it? I have to slip somebody a note now to take to the Yankee dressing room, or talk to him fast between innings. That no-fraternization rule, you know."

"You and Mantle are still pretty close, aren't you?" a writer asked.

"Sure," Billy said. "But playing against each other out there we're strangers. I'll fight him when he tries to rough me up when I try to make the double play. I'll holler it up good to the pitcher who strikes him out."

He took a .281 batting average into the Yankee Stadium on July 16th. Before hostilities began, Billy played a pepper game with Mickey Mantle's little son in front of the Yankee bench. Casey Stengel was not far away, talking with Jim Turner, his pitching coach. Billy tried to catch Old Case's eye, but the manager did not seem to relish looking his way. The lump began to form in his chest again. He wished he could make himself hate the man, but he simply could not. He was a person who could never hold a grudge. But he still could not understand how a man could cast a friend aside like an old shoe. It was the deepest injury he had ever suffered, one he knew would never fully heal. He longed to go over to Old Case and say once more, "How about it, Case. Give me an oil well, huh?"

Bill Norman started Frank Lary against the Yankees once more. For the fifth straight time the Tiger ace stopped the Bombers, this time, 12-5. Kaline, Bolling, and Maxwell led the attack against a parade of Stengel's pitchers, and Billy hit a double and scored a run. He cut down threatened Bomber rallies with a great day in the field. He had seven assists and four putouts, and made not a single miscue. He had robbed Bauer, Carey, and Berra of base hits. He had been largely responsible for giving Stengel a very unhappy afternoon.

Chapter XVIII

THE DETROIT BUBBLE burst in late July. They lost game after game and slipped fifteen and a half games out of the lead. Both Lary and Bunning had lost their magic touch against the Yankees. Both had been knocked out of the box in a fatal series in Detroit. In the three games the Bombers racked up a total of fifty runs. The Tigers could not make up for the defeats against the second-division clubs and home attendance fell off sharply. Detroit sports writers, headed by Hal Middlesworth of the *Free Press,* soon made it plain that they had given up on the Tigers, at least for 1958.

Although he was still hitting .279 and was as noisy and as scrappy as ever in the field, Billy Martin was taking the biggest share of criticism. Detroit fans had to blame somebody. They began yelling, "Ticket broker!" at him, and he wished he could call back many things he had said at the start of the season. But his great confidence in himself often back-fired. He was the first to admit he was no diplomat. Just after the pennant race got underway, he said to the writers, "I like to do favors for my friends, especially my old Yankee pals. In October I'll help get them good seats in Briggs Stadium."

He displayed not a trace of the deep disappointment he felt when any of the Detroit players were around, but when he was alone he felt a kind of despair, a doubt about the future. Too much had been expected of him. The Tigers had pinned their pennant hopes on his slight frame and his reputation as a good-luck charm.

The fans had been telling him he could no longer win with a big mouth, that he had lost whatever it was he had with the Yankees. Maybe the fans in the league had fed too long on stories of his boyish bravado, and now that he had outgrown it they were calling him an overrated ballplayer making a lot of noise to hide his lack of ability.

When he had these moments he would take the advice of a grandmother long since gone, and count his blessings. How many players would ever get into five World Series? How many kids of the thousands now playing on the sandlots would ever get into a big-league uniform? Remember, six American League clubs angled for you last winter, after hitting .251 for Kansas City! Now you're hitting .270.

He honestly thought the Tigers still had a chance to win, despite the gigantic Yankee lead. He kept telling the players that the Boston Braves, in last place on July 4th, 1914, had won the National League pennant in September. And if Detroit or any other team in the first division could have put on at least a nine-game winning streak in August, the Yankees might have been overtaken, for Stengel's club went into a woeful slump.

Bill Norman, desperately trying to find a winning

combination, put Inman "Coot" Veal, a rookie up from Birmingham, at second base and shifted Billy Martin to third. He wanted to know what Billy thought of the move.

"I played third when I was with Phoenix," he said, the old defiance burning in his eyes. "I played some third base for Kansas City. I don't care where you play me, Bill."

When he took the field against the White Sox the fans began jeering him.

"So they gave up on you, hot shot?" a fan yelled. "It's about time."

"Veal on second!" another shouted. "Ham on third!" Laughter rippled through the stands. When he came into the dugout, Reno Bertoia said, "I wouldn't blame you if you climbed into the stands and went after them."

"They pay to come here and boo me," Billy said, his voice shaking a little as he spoke.

He faced Donovan in the second inning and hit him for a single, but was forced at second when Veal hit to Aparicio. Sherman Lollar's grand-slam homer in the fifth put the White Sox out in front and kept them there. Billy got his second hit in the eighth, but could not be moved around. Out of twelve hits off Donovan, the Tigers could score only three runs. They lost, 9-3, and slipped eighteen and a half games out of first place.

Billy could not remember when he'd seen a more dispirited bunch of ballplayers. He refused to go down into the dumps with them. "We're not dead yet!" he told them. "We've got the rest of this month and all of September to make a comeback. We've got as much chance as five other clubs to take second place. Nearly two thousand dollars will buy a lot of steaks."

The next afternoon he tried to prove to the fans in Briggs Stadium that he still scrambled for every inch of advantage despite the fifth-place position of the Tigers. In the eighth inning he got to third on a walk, a sacrifice, and a fly ball, and with the weak end of the batting order coming up, tried to steal home.

He collided with Earl Battey, catching for the White Sox, and felt a stabbing pain in his side. Getting up slowly, he looked at Billy Hoeft, waiting to hit, and shook his head. Jack Hormel hurried out of the dugout and Billy said, "My ribs hurt." He took a deep breath and a grimace of pain spread over his face. Sweat glistened on his forehead. "Looks like I cracked something, Jack."

In the clubhouse, after an examination by the club physician, Billy was told there was no evidence of a fracture, but that he'd be side-lined for at least a week.

"I guess I don't live right," Billy choked out. "What else can happen to me?"

Stewing over his inactivity, he sat on the bench and watched Bunning beat the Athletics, 3-2. Mostly his eyes were on Veal and Bertoia, for he knew one or both of them could be with the Tigers as a regular next year.

Without him, Detroit won five straight, and Coot Veal was turning in a sparkling game at short and beginning to pick up with the bat. Misgivings began to stir inside Billy, but first of all he was a team man. He was the loudest in praise of Veal and Bertoia. He talked with them over mistakes they made in the field, and tipped them off about certain pitching deliveries and when to expect them.

When the Tigers reached Cleveland, Billy said to Norman, "I'll be able to play today or tomorrow if you need me."

"Take your time, Billy," the manager said, a twinkle in his eye as he glanced at Al Kaline. "You're not as young as you used to be." Quickly he added, "You're doing a pretty good job where you are."

Norman's remark ruffled Billy's temper but he got himself in hand. Five years ago he would have blown sky-high.

Whatever slim outside chance the Tigers might have had was washed out in Kansas City where they lost three in a row. Billy stormed and fumed in the locker room, raving over what might have been. Up in Boston, the Red Sox swept a series with the Yankees. "They've been playing under-five-hundred baseball all month," he yelled. "We should be a lot closer to the Yankees."

He had played third for Norman in two of the games and had knocked out two singles. His average was .268.

Ernest Mehl of the Kansas City *Star* waved a plastic helmet at the downcast infielder. " 'Billy the Kid' it says inside," he called out. "Say, Billy, did you really invent this gimmick for these hard hats?"

"Sure," he said. "It was simple. I just attached sponge-rubber extensions to the lining and they're about two inches long and an inch wide and they come down over a player's temples like Elvis Presley sideburns. I always wondered why they weren't given those things in the first place. Look at the added protection you've got if you're hit." He grinned and turned the plastic helmet over and over in his hand. He began laughing. "Maybe I'll get a patent out and become a millionaire. In about twenty years I could be rich."

"We'll be in Yankee Stadium on Sunday, the twenty-fifth," Norman said, coming over. "I'd like to sweep that double-header. On Saturday night, Billy, I want you to keep Mantle and that Whitey Ford out late. Until about six o'clock Sunday morning."

"Hey!" Billy laughed. "Wouldn't that make Weiss jump?"

It was a hot Sunday afternoon in New York. The old bitterness crept into Billy Martin when he began limbering up before the game. Some of the fans hooted at him, but the majority of them had not forgotten the days when he had performed so brilliantly for Stengel. They let him know it when he hit Ditmar for a single in the first inning, driving in Detroit's first run. They applauded a stop he made close to the third-base bag in the second. His throw got Siebern by a step. From the bench in the Detroit dugout he hurled defiance at the Yankees. While playing third, he tormented Crosetti, the Yankee coach.

Detroit won the first game easily, 8-3, but Shantz won the nightcap, 3-2 for the Bombers. Despite the fact that he had made two more hits and fielded brilliantly, he raged in the showers. "Four hits they get. Not one off Moford in seven innings. We had it sewed up, and then that Siebern gets lucky and hits one into the short right-field seats. Did those Yankees today look like a team that wins pennants? I ask you!"

The driving needles of the shower took some of the sting of defeat out of him, and he looked forward with thanks for tomorrow's open date. His ribs were still tender and in a few minutes he'd give his sore leg muscle the whirlpool treatment. There were thirty-two games left to play, another 154 next year. And the next?

He had to think ahead. He needed at least three more years to assure his little daughter's future and his sister's education. His mother must never again know the poverty of the old days and he was determined that Alfred Manuel "Billy" Martin would continue to enjoy the best there was in life. He'd had a taste of strawberry shortcake with whipped cream and he certainly did not want to go back to stewed prunes.

On September 1st the Tigers had won sixty-one games and lost sixty-five. Now they concentrated on overhauling the second-place White Sox and the third-place Red Sox. But they could not get going. Billy's hitting fell off, for he just couldn't get the leverage he needed from his bad leg when he took his swings at the plate. Norman benched him along with Bertoia.

When the fans and the sports writers criticized Norman, Billy replied with complete justification, "I never posed as a leader or called myself one. A lot of you guys did. Leading is a manager's job. I was and still am a good second baseman. Nobody can deny that. Even Stengel doesn't. I never claimed to be as good at short or third!"

The sports writers had him at the end of the trail.

What a pity, they said. His fire had burned out. But men who made baseball their business knew better, and just after the baseball meetings in Chicago, the news leaked out that Frank Lane, general manager of the Cleveland Indians, was going to try and make a deal for him in 1959. He would give up Narleski, the fireball pitcher, and the veteran Vic Wertz to get Billy for second base.

"I'll even throw in a utility infielder if I have to," he was quoted as saying. "If I'd been able to get Martin last fall, we'd be in a much better position in the league than we are now."

Kansas City wanted him back too. The Washington Senators and Baltimore Orioles admitted they would talk business during the winter if it concerned Billy Martin.

His confidence returned, helped along by a statement by his manager. Norman said Billy had done all that had been expected of him and was the kind of player he wanted to keep on his ball club. "So old Billy is through, is he? But it seems some ball clubs don't think so, and their judgment ought to be better than that of the writers."

When Reno Bertoia failed to hit and became uncertain in the field, Billy took over third base again. Despite his incessant prodding, the Tigers could not seem to win. Even Lary and Bunning could not last nine innings on the pitching mound.

The Tigers faced Billy Pierce at Comiskey Park in Chicago on April 24th. A win for the White Sox meant they would clinch second place. "This one," Billy said in the locker room as he changed into his uniform, "is one we've got to win. We can still finish second if we do."

Bill Norman started Frank Lary against Pierce and batted Billy in the seventh spot in the line-up. It was one of the best-played games of the season, and anybody's game going into the tenth inning. Billy had made two hits off Pierce when he stepped up in the ninth. He worked the count to two balls and one strike, then slashed his third single into left field.

Coot Veal was an easy out, and then Norman sent big Gus Zernial up to hit for Lary. Pierce walked the pinch batter and sent Billy to second. Harvey Kuenn flied out and Billy kicked dirt up and yelled in at Detroit's catcher, Red Wilson: "Bring us around, Red. Get hold of one!"

Wilson drove a hit through the infield and Billy came in to score. Again he had delivered a hit and scored a run in a key game when it was sorely needed. After a conference on the mound, Billy Pierce walked off and Moore replaced him. The relief pitcher set Al Kaline down and the White Sox came in to hit. Tom Morgan took the mound for Bill Norman and got the side out and the game went into the tenth inning.

Moore had been taken out for a pinch-hitter in the ninth for Chicago, and a rookie pitcher named Rudolph easily disposed of the Tiger hitters in the top of the tenth.

Landis, a power hitter, who had come into the White Sox line-up in the eighth, greeted Tom Morgan with a triple, and Billy raced in to talk to Morgan. The crowd, one of the smallest of the year, hooted and jeered. "Don't give Lollar anything too good," Billy warned. "Landis is the only guy that counts right now. Bear down!"

Morgan threw one in that *was* too good and Sherman Lollar, always a dangerous hitter, slashed it over short to drive in Landis. Now there would be a struggle for third place in the league between Boston, Detroit, and Cleveland.

In the locker room, Billy choked back his disappointment and shouted at the dispirited Tigers, "Third-place money can also buy a lot of things!"

He did not let down for a single minute during the last week of the pennant race, and showed the fans he was still a hungry and ambitious ballplayer. His courage and fierce pride kept him in the line-up despite the leg muscle that seldom failed to bother him.

On the final day of the season Ray Narleski beat Detroit and dropped them into fifth place. The Tiger, its tail twisted, slunk into the dressing room and felt like crawling under the lockers. In the loss of three out of the last four games with the Indians, Detroit had scored just seven runs in thirty-six innings and had left forty-two men on base. During the last thirteen home games the fans in Detroit had shown their disgust with the Tigers. A total of about seventy thousand fans had turned out during that time, a crowd that would not quite fill Yankee Stadium on a single afternoon.

The most disconsolate player in the visitors' dressing room was Billy Martin. To Bob Greene of the Detroit

News and other writers he said, "Tell 'em I'm sorry I did not win the pennant for them." He meant the fans. Now he was the nervous, brooding little man again, the one who found it almost impossible to accept defeat at anything. "Tell them that, for I really am." Looking as miserable as a man can, he shook his head sadly and stared down at the floor. "I felt I was getting to be a pretty good shortstop when they moved me."

He did not mean it as an alibi and the Cleveland writers knew it. One of them quickly came to his defense: "They played you out of position all year and the fans expected miracles from you, Billy."

"All year we ran hot and cold," Billy said. "Somehow we always managed to let the fans down." He walked around, sat down, and as quickly got to his feet again.

As he said good-byes, he wondered if he would be with these guys again next year. His future, it seemed, depended on the winter trades. Would his .255 batting average with the Tigers change the minds of the traders? He had a talk with Bill Norman on the way to Detroit and asked him to put the facts on the line.

"No double-talk, Bill," Billy said. "I've had too much of that since I left the Yankees."

"Frank Lane has been saying I'm going to let you go, but not me, Billy. As far as I'm concerned, you'll be going to Lakeland next spring. I'm figuring on shifting Bertoia to the outfield next year and making a deal for a third baseman. I'd like to keep Veal at short, so that leaves second base to you."

"It's where I belong, Bill. It's home," Billy said.

Chapter XIX

IN DETROIT, while Billy was packing his things for the trip back to Berkeley, his mind was far from being at ease. The strange truth was that, despite the supreme confidence in himself, he had never really felt secure in baseball. Even when he was riding high for the Yankees. "Some of us can be happy playing ball," he told Mickey Mantle when they'd started rooming together. "But I've never been able to get a grip on myself in this business. Sometimes I get depressed and have a hard time getting out of those spells."

All ballplayers have to face one hard, cold fact as their productive years roll by. They have to realize the solid wisdom of the old saying about the spirit being willing but the flesh weak. For him it could come next year, or the next. The pressure of his early years, the long struggle to rise above poverty, and then the battle to meet the competition of the big leagues had left their marks on him. But his fighting spirit would never diminish.

Billy's many friends would be the first to tell him he had nothing to worry about. Although baseball had been his very life since he had been big enough to swing a bat, they were positive he would be a success at any other line of work.

Whether it was Detroit again next year or any other club, he would give his level best, for he knew no other way to work at anything. He tried not to think of the possibility of his going back to the minor leagues. He knew his pride would not allow it. He'd rather quit baseball.

A man of rapidly changing moods, Billy shed all his gloomy thoughts when he finally walked up the steps of the Martin home and grinned at his sister who was waiting in the doorway.

"It's Billy, Mother!" Joanie shouted.

Secure in the warmth of his happy family circle, he realized how good baseball had been to him and for all those around him; and all he asked for now, prayed for, was just enough time to finish all he had planned for them.

The 1958 World Series convinced Billy that the Yankees were not the team they used to be. "The Braves should have won," he said to his old friends one afternoon in Al Faccini's place. "My old pal, Whitey Ford, I'm sorry to say, doesn't look like he'll go far next year. Who really won the series for Stengel? Old Hank Bauer. Without him the Yanks would've been lucky to win two games. The Yankees are ready to go into a spin and I think I'll be in another World Series yet."

He sat back and waited for the trade winds to blow.

The one that came his way was warm and sweet. During the second week of November he was notified that he had been traded to the Cleveland Indians for Narleski, Mossi and Alvarez. He was as jubilant as he had been that day the Oakland club sent him to the Yankees. He felt as young. The most significant part of the transaction was that Frank Lane had beaten three other American League clubs to the deal. Again it was made plainly clear that baseball-wise men knew that Billy Martin had more to offer than what appeared in the batting and fielding averages.

Statistics could not correctly measure the talents of this kind of ballplayer. Hustle, a winning spirit, and dead gameness were paying off.

Even Casey Stengel told reporters at the time, "He's a professional, that fella. Put him anywhere and he'll do a job for you."

No ballplayer can receive a bigger compliment than to be called a professional. Stengel's statement convinced thousands of fans all over the country that he still kept a warm place in his heart for Billy Martin. Perhaps they had never wanted to believe otherwise.

Lane announced later that he had obtained Jimmy Piersall from the Boston Red Sox for Vic Wertz and a bonus rookie, Gary Geiger. He intended to convert Larry Doby into a first baseman.

"Colavito, Piersall, and Minnie Minoso in the outfield," Billy said when reporters interviewed him. "Vic Power, Doby, Woody Held, and me in the infield. They still have Mickey Vernon, and Herb Score should make a comeback. That's a great ball club and the Yankees won't run away with it next year. I could easily get into the World Series."

Think so and it will be!

If Billy does — and who would bet against him? — a lot of people, even in New York, will be happy; for there are only a handful of players left in the game with his spirit, his flair for stirring up excitement. He is just about the last of the Eddie Stanky and Leo Durocher school. When he does pass out of the picture — and take his word for it, he is nowhere near ready yet — the fans will realize how important he was to the game of baseball and will sorely miss him.

A more colorful and inspiring figure, a more dedicated ballplayer, will never be recorded in the annals of baseball.

BILLY MARTIN

Born: May 16, 1928   Height: 5' 11½"   Weight: 165   Bats and throws right

Year	Club	League	Pos.	G	AB	R	H	2B	3B	HR	RBI	BA	PO	A	E	FA
1946	Idaho Falls	Pion.	2B-3B	32	114	13	29	7	0	0	12	.254	33	55	16	.846
1947	Phoenix	A-T	3B	130	586	141	230	48	12	9	174	.392	207	317	55	.905
1947	Oakland	P. C.	2B-3B	15	53	3	12	3	0	0	23	.226	23	24	5	.904
1948	Oakland	P. C.	INF	132	401	60	111	28	2	3	42	.277	301	288	21	.966
1949	Oakland	P. C.	2B-SS	172	623	90	178	27	3	12	92	.286	454	475	37	.962
1950	Kansas City	A. A.	2B	29	118	15	33	6	2	4	10	.280	68	80	8	.949
1950	New York	A. L.	2B-SS	34	36	10	9	1	0	1	8	.250	24	16	1	.976
1951	New York	A. L.	INF-OF	51	58	10	15	1	2	0	2	.259	45	62	4	.964
1952	New York	A. L.	2B	109	363	32	97	13	3	3	33	.267	244	323	9	.984
1953	New York	A. L.	2B-SS	149	587	72	151	24	6	15	75	.257	389	409	14	.983
1954									(In Military Service)							
1955	New York	A. L.	2B-SS	20	70	8	21	2	0	1	9	.300	46	50	3	.970
1956	New York	A. L.	2B-3B	121	458	76	121	24	5	9	49	.264	253	288	15	.973
1957	N. Y.-K. C.	A. L.	2B-3B	116	410	45	103	14	5	10	39	.250	220	232	13	.972
1958	Detroit	A. L.	SS-3B	131	498	56	127	19	1	7	42	.255	206	288	20	.965
Major League Totals				731	2480	309	644	98	22	46	257	.259	1427	1668	79	.973

WORLD SERIES RECORD

Year	Club	League	Pos.	G	AB	R	H	2B	3B	HR	RBI	BA	PO	A	E	FA
1951	New York	A. L.	PR	1	0	1	0	0	0	0	0	.000	0	0	0	.000
1952	New York	A. L.	2B	7	23	2	5	0	0	1	4	.217	16	16	1	.970
1953	New York	A. L.	2B	6	24	5	12	1	2	2	8	.500	13	14	0	1.000
1955	New York	A. L.	2B	7	25	2	8	1	1	0	4	.320	17	20	0	1.000
1956	New York	A. L.	2B-3B	7	27	5	8	2	2	3	3	.296	14	20	0	1.000
World Series Totals				28	99	15	33	4	5	6	19	.333	60	70	1	.990

Index

189

About the Author

JOE ARCHIBALD was born in Portsmouth, New Hampshire, and after graduating from high school there spent nearly two years at the Academy of Fine Arts in Chicago determined to become a sports cartoonist. After six months as a police reporter on a Boston newspaper, he came to New York City where he was hired as a sports cartoonist for a small newspaper syndicate. Later he worked for the McClure Newspaper Syndicate and the United Feature Syndicate where his cartoons and sports copy appeared in over a hundred newspapers. He gave up cartooning for writing and has attained popularity as a writer of sport fiction and biography for boys.

92
Martin